TECHNOLOGY AND LABOUR

TECHNOLOGY AND LABOUR

Selected Essays

BHASKAR MAJUMDER

PUBLICATIONS

KALPAZ PUBLICATIONS

DELHI-110052

Technology and Labour : Selected Essays

Rs. 590

ISBN: 81-7835-613-9

Published in 2007 in India by
Kalpaz Publications
C-30, Satyawati Nagar,
Delhi-110052
E-mail: kalpaz@hotmail.com
Phone : 9212729499

Lasser Type Setting by: Rudra Computer Graphics, Delhi
Printed at : Salasar Imaging System, Delhi

Contents

Preface

Land, labour and capital are the visible means of production of commodities, but technology is the invisible means without which no commodity can be produced. Technology is what distinguishes one stage of production and development from another since it reflects the level of creativity and innovation of each stage. However technology also has a destructive role since it often leads to the replacement of labour by capital, leading to retrenchment and displacement of workers. In this book, which is a collection of selected papers on labour and technology published in a number of journals since 1991, I have tried to explore the creative and destructive role of technology for labour employment and displacement. The papers include both theoretical and applied issues. The applied issues are based on empirical data collected from selected regions in India. Some of the data is of the distant past but I believe they are relevant even today for understanding the problems that I have tried to focus on. The papers cover both voluntary and forced labour and both single and multiple jobs. Most of the rural poor who work as labourers are engaged in multiple jobs to earn support income for survival rather than for job diversification. Additionally, both migration and mobility of labour have been considered; migration has been considered as both voluntary and forced while mobility has been considered as inter-firm, inter-sectoral and inter-regional.

While considering technology, we considered capital-output ratios by both theoretical possibilities and empirical data. We also considered the market-technology association and hence the possibilities of growth and development, particularly in the context of a developing economy like India. The role of the state has come into the analysis for protection of displaceable labourers following technological improvement unaccompanied by market expansion. The protection by rehabilitation of the labourers employed earlier has been taken care of by analysis on the role of the state.

The book being a collection of essays can not offer all the aspects that are relevant and necessary for covering issues on labour and technology. Nevertheless, the book has tried to offer and analyze issues that will carry meaning for the researchers on the theme.

Allahabad
April 2007

Bhaskar Majumder

Introduction

An obvious geometrical-biological fact of nature is that no single force can generate any outcome. For something to happen in the physical world, there has to exist two opposite non-parallel forces. The struggle between these two opposite non-parallel forces produces a result that may be either positive or negative. Development may also be considered to be the struggle of the opposites. In this case the two forces are human beings and the productive forces of nature. The relationship between them, which may be interactive or conflicting, yields output, which then leads to development. In the literature developed by Adam Smith, these productive forces are land, labour and capital. These are the wealth of nations distributed as rent, wages and profit. In the literature developed by Marx, labour and capital are in a conflicting relation, with the conflict between them expressed as the benefits of output distributed as wages and profits. In both the cases, capital conquests over land and labour, though capital as a means of production to produce commodities is a transformation of land by application of labour.

For this transformation to take place that will result in the production of commodities, use of technology, which is the invisible human factor that evolves as human beings progress, is a pre-condition. Production of commodities may be taken as the domain that gives expression to technology, while human labour and man-transformed resources are the means by which technology is expressed. Technological progress leads to changing skill requirement, which offers the scope for additional labour employment. On the other hand, obsolescence of technology leads to redundancy and exit of existing labour. These and other issues revolving around commodity production, technology and labour, especially the relationship between them, are the focus of the present book. The book is a collection of eleven essays around the theme 'Technology and Labour', which focus on production of commodities and their relationship with technology and labour. The common thread running through the papers is that technology is both the cause and consequence of labour absorption and labour displacement. The contexts of the papers range from local to global and the issues relating technology and labour have been posed in the context of a developing economy. The essays are based on both theoretical and applied studies. The theoretical essays are based on specific assumptions depending on the specific purpose of the essay. For example, in some of the essays it is shown that technological progress-led labour redundancy is labour (knowledge) made, while capital takes advantage of it by non-realization (non-marketing) of higher volume of physical output produced. In fact, as explained in some of the papers, capital ownership-cum-accumulation, via market constraint, declares redundancy of labour. Elimination (exit) of a section of workers by rationalization of the firm or downsizing can not solve the problem, because it would accentuate market constraint unless compensated by sunrise industries. Some of the papers focus on the unavoidable relative obsolescence of the labourers at some point in time because of technological advancement. Some of the essays try to assert that the task for rehabilitation of workers rests on the workers, managers and extra-plant authorities, e.g, institutions and the state. These tasks, as explained, revolve around education, training, job rotation etc. The applied studies center both on case studies like that of rickshaw pullers in the city of Allahabad in Uttar Pradesh and on the often shifting state-cum-national level location of the labourers. Some of the papers have tried to deal with the question on identification of the labourers engaged in multiple jobs and hence earning income from a number of sources in addition to time spent on those jobs. Thus, the essays also deal with the migration and mobility factors at the regional level. Forced labour or involuntary employment of labour vis-à-vis diversification of occupations in the informal sector has also been dealt with in some of the papers. While the essays explore the possibilities of labour employment, they also put forward technological progress-led redundancy of labourers and hence the question of rehabilitation of the labourers facing exit. Thus technology is seen in two ways, one labour displacing and the other labour absorbing.

In the stages of development, land by its inelasticity in use for production purposes shows its ultimate limitations, so that the leaders in the domain of production move forward in terms of land-saving devices. The technique of production gradually shifts from being land-using and labour-using to capital-using. While it shows material-saving in production, a movement from production of heavy weight goods to light weight goods, it also shows a shift from agriculture (land-based activities) to industry. Hence, the same forward movement (development) also shows displacement of workers from rural (agricultural sector) to urban (industrial-cum-services) areas (sectors). Development invites challenges from those thus displaced.

While feudalism (pre-capitalist stage) shows inclusion and exclusion of cross-sections of society by social indicators like caste, community, colour, language, gender etc., capitalism shows inclusion and exclusion by economic indicators like income, assets, wage-employment etc. Thus, while in case of the former we find (in) human face, in case of the latter that face itself is absent since it is person/preference neutral. Hence, the logic/discourse of development that is relevant for a capitalist economy will be not much relevant (if not totally irrelevant) for a feudal economy although undeniably capitalist economy took birth in the womb of a feudal economy. In fact an economy under capitalist transition will have many of the feudal parameters present in its functioning.

The central question of the different stages of development is who owns and controls resources. In case of primitive communism, it was collective/group control (through hunting, collecting etc). In case of slavery, it was the master buying and selling (controlling) slaves. Both the master and the slaves were human beings of different colours. In case of feudalism, it was landlord controlling land (major means of production) and hence employing tenants at will. There came indirect control of one section of people over the other sections. In case of capitalism, it is the owners of capital that control owners of labour-power. In each of these stages, it is technology that plays a vital role in differentiating one stage from the other.

The total separation of the productive forces (labour) from the means of production (non-labour) corresponds to a higher state of technology and higher stage of development. In fact the separation gets sharpened under capitalism, reflecting a post-private property scenario where a section appropriates the fruits of labour by accumulating capital, controlling capital and using it for both accommodation and destruction of labour. The better the technology (implying higher labour productivity), the more the chances of employment of 'new labour' (called skilled by latest technology) and obsolescence (exit) of 'old labour'. If the 'new labour' (by number of labourers) cannot outnumber the 'old labour', the time-series outcome will be net eviction from the domain of capital-dependent production.

While as a process industrialization shows labour struggle, as a phenomenon and a consequence, it shows a forward movement from lower-order goods to higher-order goods. It also shows a movement from low-tech to high-tech goods, though the technology-goods association is not always linear. The economic identity of a worker is that he may be mainly an agricultural worker or mainly an industrial worker, if we confine ourselves to the domain of material production. There is no conflict between these two types of workers; two workers may co-exist. The problem comes when one is abruptly told to leave the earlier job where he developed his skill over time. The suggested exit of the labourer may be because of his relative obsolescence. This also shows a movement from simple social division of labour to complex economic division of labour. In the first case the division is often caste-cum-gender based, while in case of the latter it is competence-training based. The former is less formal or even informal (family/heredity based) while the latter is formal (institution-based).

For a number of reasons the sections that become victims in the forward movement of technology-cum-production are the people at the bottom of the socio-economic ladder. By consequence the reasons are low income, low land holding, absence of productive assets, etc. However the causes may be the multiple boundaries by which the initial non-privileged or underprivileged are obstructed from entering into the domain of privileges. The boundaries are erected by literacy and education, elite language (English), caste (that is a dominant factor in some regions in India), community, height-weight-colour of the person, gender (in some regions), access to institutions, holding posts of power etc. The additional factors that perpetuate vulnerability of the bottommost sections are less information, low mobility and tradition-custom-belief constraint. As a corollary, the people at the bottom of the power structure are unable to calculate the way they should resist/withstand the pressure of change from land-based to capital-based economic activities. In any conflict between land and capital, capital takes the upper hand by being more mobile and under the control of the more competent people in a political system. These people in their turn are controlled by the capital owners in an economic system of capitalism.

A linear and single path of development that was followed by the countries now called industrialized is often confused as the path of development to be followed by all countries. But for geo-political-economic-cultural reasons this path may be neither desirable nor feasible since a particular country or a region within a country may choose to remain slow in growth and move on the pre-industrial path. There may also be differences in development visualized by cross-sections of population simultaneous to the development envisaged by the country as a whole. In addition there may also emerge inter-temporal differential in strategies in development. Thus a single straitjacket path of development may not fit all the countries for all times to come. Most of the countries in the Third World have remained, by choice or by compulsion, less industrialized relative to the countries in west Europe, North America and Japan.

Local people and natural resources along with local culture and local conditions are some factors that influence development. If these factors are taken into consideration while planning the path of development of an economy, it leads to inclusive development, which is the best path of growth. As opposed to this, if growth is imposed on people in a condition where the benefits of growth fail to be shared equally among all, a large section of the population is excluded from the benefits of development, which is a highly undesirable situation. In this book we argue not against growth per se, but against exclusive growth. The book accepts the proposition that production of commodities is a reflection of social cooperation, whatever is the state of technology. Hence, what we have accepted is that a process of growth visible to all has to be shared by all. Based on this, the book also focuses on a type of growth that is output-employment oriented and home market dependent. The papers in the book stress on development and use of need-based technology because technology is useful for converting community and caste based social isolation into production-based interdependence. For this technology, and not just the ownership over resources, will determine the path of growth of the economy.

1

Commodity Production and Command: Some Observations

The concern of economists for production-centered economic analysis is as old as the birth of economics as a branch of scientific analysis (Chakravarty 1988; Hicks, 1965, p. 36-48; Hicks, 1971, p. 15-24; Kuznets, 1961, p. 13; Kuznets, 1965, p. 63, 83, 84, 105; Kerr, 1993, p. 5, 9). Production shows a domain where natural resources are transformed by human labour to yield products. The products, having use-value, become commodities by acquiring the property of exchange-value. The combined values, namely, use-value and exchange-value, show the concrete shape of production, that is, commodities. The link between natural resources and human labour as cause and commodities as final output is technology. Commodity can also be seen as the concrete shape of technology.

In general, commodity is the sphere where economic categories like production, exchange, distribution, and consumption take shape. The major economic problems, and hence objectives and strategies, like attainment of economic self-reliance, removal of poverty, attaining full-employment, ensuring basic needs of life etc. are integrally linked with these economic categories. It is clear by now that the positive volume of physical output of commodities and positive rate of growth of output may fail to ensure the above objectives. A fresh look, thus, is necessary on the question of commodity production not only to examine the technological dimensions of economic growth, but also to examine if economic agents who are the cause and consequence of growth can ensure that growth.

We take a national economy as the unit of analysis in this paper. The axioms for this purpose are the following:

Axiom 1 : Each capable individual gets involved in commodity production as her/his own compulsion (need-based). This production is social (exchange-based) also, as her/his own compulsion. The rest of the society is not visibly compelling any particular individual to produce excess for others.

Axiom 2 : Initial labour-power applied, or labour-time spent by the particular individual, on nature denotes development of tools and techniques to help her/his production operations in the succeeding periods. Development of human knowledge by 'doing' shows introduction and development of technologies.

Axiom 3 : Exchange of commodities among individuals initially denotes a kind of agreement among the individuals, keeping in mind labour-time required to produce commodities exchanged.

Axiom 4 : Development of tools and techniques alter the capability parameters of the individuals, e.g., changed labour-time required to produce the initial commodity. This technology-differential, as it widens, leads to command-differential and hence come new set of commodities.

Given the above axioms, we analyze in Section I of this paper the basic ideas on commodity production and command of the economic agents over commodities produced. In Section II, we analyze the nature of consensus on commodity production. In Section III, we link production, command, and development, which constitute at the same time, the concluding part of this paper.

I. Commodity Production

It is known that the problems like unemployment, poverty, inequality, inflation, foreign debt etc., are rooted in issues related to production of commodities. At the beginning there was an unknown world yet to be explored by man. The urge for survival or initial material existence compelled him to transform nature (observable and accessible to him) by application of his labour-power. Initial output was produced by man independent of his own choice and independent of the question of any consensus. It was the individual compulsion which became a social phenomenon because of (i) the inability of the individual to produce all the commodities he needs; (ii) the choice-neutrality of any particular individual in the sense that if (i) holds good, he will have to produce in excess for others and hence exchange. At the same time, it is a fact that location of individuals in the production map shows the location of the same individuals in the consumption map. The latter, viz., the relative command of individuals over commodities produced may not satisfy all individuals equally. This command-differential ultimately leads to questioning the nature of commodity production and growth path.

How does command-differential come? The application of technology at the dawn of history, e.g., in the era of hunting, did not yield any questionable command-differential. During that period, production was in terms of ability of an individual, but sharing was in terms of need. 'Questionable command-differential' is derived from ' resource differential': unequal resources owned and transformed by the resource-owners in the domain of production of commodities. Natural resources are generally non-renewable, and, subject to knowledge of engineering, substitutable in production of commodities. Manpower or quality-weighted labour force transforms nature to yield output. Non-labour resources like land and machinery did not exist in a vacuum; while land is known to be a direct part of nature, machinery is 'past labour exercised on nature' maintained for re-use in production of a new set of commodities. The higher the stage of production of commodities the higher is the importance of non-labour resources and the lower is the significance of land and sometimes labour. However, it is the owner of labour, viz., the labourer who opens up the technological options for unlimited economic growth of the globe on an infinite time sequence.

Thus, the commodity-technology association for the economy can be written as:

$$\{Q, T\} \cong \{Q_i, T_j\} \quad \begin{matrix} i = 1, \dots n \\ j = 1, \dots m \end{matrix} \qquad \dots(1)$$

where Q is a vector of produceable commodities and T is a vector of technologies in production of Q.

Here, $m \geq n$, on the assumption of non-identical technology for any two commodities. T denotes the nature of association between human (labour) and non-human resources. While Q is constrained to move along a single product curve, T is an operator that explains the shift of the curve. T covers certain characteristics like 'scale of operations', nature of the products etc. (Stewart, 1977). Q and T are determined simultaneously. It is not that the economic agents will have to produce all the n produceable commodities (resource-technology specifying) at a particular period of time. It may choose to produce any subset of the whole.

Starting with a simple two-individual (A_1 and A_2) two-commodity (Q_1 and Q_2) case, one can obtain production strategy as follows:

The production of commodities reflects autonomous behaviour of both A and B. Then one arrives at their respective 'command positions' and possibility of 'command-differential'. Let us use an example:

Example: 1

Economic Agents	A_1	A_2
Technology in Use	T_1	T_2

Production of Commodities	Q_1	Q_2
Self-Use	Q_{11}	Q_{22}
Excess for Exchange	Q_{12}	Q_{21}
Exchanged Commodities	Q_{21}	Q_{12}
Command Position	(Q_{11}, Q_{21})	(Q_{12}, Q_{22})

Let there be equivalence in exchange in terms of a numeraire; it can be any of the two commodities. So one takes $Q_{12} \approx Q_{21} > 0$ for interdependence and hence for exchange to occur, thus, showing existence of A and B in social production.

In this system

$$Q_1 = Q_{11} + Q_{12} \quad .....(2)$$

$$Q_2 = Q_{21} + Q_{22} \quad .... (3)$$

Let C_1 and C_2 denote positions of individuals A_1 and A_2 respectively in total output (Q_1, Q_2). Then

$$C_1 \equiv (Q_{11}, Q_{21}),\ Q_{11} \geq 0,\ Q_{21} > 0 \quad .... (4)$$

$$C_2 \equiv (Q_{12}, Q_{22}),\ Q_{22} \geq 0,\ Q_{12} > 0 \quad .... (5)$$

The system generates the same level of output for each period with a given state of technology specific to a given commodity produced by a single economic agent.

There is no category as households selling labour to firms. The economic agents are producers, employing their own labour (not hired) and non-labour resources (part of nature) accessible to them. Resource constraint is assumed away. So one obtains a production system as a characterization of interdependence among the producers. These producers become consumers in a post-exchange situation.

Let individual A_3 join the system producing Q_3. It is also an autonomous decision, out of which his self-use is Q_{33}, so that (6) is the necessary condition for existence of A_3 in social production, where Q_{31} and Q_{32} are portions of Q_3 required by A_1 and A_2 respectively. Now if none of them need Q_3, then A_3 fails to participate in social production. The implication is, production of commodities independent of requirements by the rest of the society does not ensure command of the particular individual behaving autonomously in production of commodities.

$$Q_3 - Q_{33} = Q_{31} + Q_{32}, \qquad Q_{33} \geq 0; Q_{31}, Q_{32} > 0 \text{ .... (6)}$$

Now in a situation where a commodity produced by an individual is required by the other, the 'relative command positions' are derived in a post-exchange situation. With repetition of T_1 by A_1 and T_2 by A_2, there does not come any command-differential, on the assumption of maintenance of equivalence in exchange. Even if money is introduced to work only as a medium of exchange, this equivalence in exchange is not disturbed. How does command-differential come then?

Accepting $Q_{12} \approx Q_{21} > 0$, the same initial technologies are unlikely to be repeated in producing Q_1 and/or Q_2. If both A_1 and A_2 move technologically upward to produce more of Q_1 and Q_2, there is a chance that the equality $\lambda Q_{12} = \lambda Q_{21}$, $\lambda > 1$ is ensured, denoting reducing labour-time required to produce commodities following technological progress. However, technological progress in production of commodities by A_1 and A_2 are unlikely to be equal (or at the same rate) so that non-equivalence in exchange and in command position comes again. The point is that inter-firm technology-differential via generation of surplus or deficit output (relative to what is required by the rest of the agents) leads to the ultimate command-differential. Obviously this command-differential is a post-exchange phenomenon.

In an n-commodity frame, with one commodity being produced by one individual having a single non-identical technology, the 'relative command positions' and 'command-differentials' are derived for n individuals.

Let the n commodities be Q_1, Q_2 ..... Q_n decided to be produced by n individuals A_1, A_2, ... A_n, with associated technologies T_1, T_2, ... T_n. Here T_1 is one specific way of converting natural resources by A_1 to produce Q_1 (consumable and tradable). T_1 is the 'best available' technology among alternative technologies and by application becomes best-practiced technology for Q_1. Similarly for T_2, ..., T_n. Thus, in this n-commodity frame, the command-position for individuals A_1, A_2, ..., A_n are as follows:

In this the sharing of output shows the command position by the agents participating in production as the following:

Economic Agents	***Product and Associated Technology***	***Command***
A_1	(Q_1, T_1)	C_1
A_2	(Q_2, T_2)	C_2
-	-	-
-	-	-
A_n	(Q_n, T_n)	C_n

$$C_1 \equiv (Q_{11}, Q_{21}, \ldots, Q_{n1}), \quad Q_{11} \geq 0, (Q_{21}, \ldots Q_{n1}) > 0$$

$$C_2 \equiv (Q_{12}, Q_{22}, \ldots, Q_{n2}), \quad Q_{22} \geq 0, (Q_{12}, Q_{32}, \ldots Q_{n2}) > 0 \quad \ldots\ldots (7)$$

$$C_n \equiv (Q_{1n}, Q_{2n}, \ldots Q_{nn}), \quad Q_{nn} \geq 0, (Q_{1n}, \ldots, Q_{n-1,n}) > 0$$

Also the output and its alternative uses are stated as:

$$Q_1 = Q_{11} + Q_{12} + \ldots + Q_{1n}, \quad Q_{11} \geq 0, \quad \sum_{j=2}^{n} Q_{1i} > 0$$

$$Q_2 = Q_{21} + Q_{22} + \ldots + Q_{2n}, \quad Q_{21} \geq 0, \quad \sum_{j=1, j\neq 2}^{n} Q_{2i} > 0 \quad \ldots\ldots (8)$$

$$Q_n = Q_{n1} + Q_{n2} + \ldots + Q_{nn}, \quad Q_{nn} \geq 0, \quad \sum_{k=1}^{n-1} Q_{nk} > 0$$

With the same state of technology continued by the individuals in production of commodities, and equivalence in exchange being unchanged, when one individual produces one single commodity, command-differential does not come. With respect to technological change there come changing levels of output and hence command-differential. Market as the context of exchange, or price mechanism, could alter the initial exchange equivalence. The point is that money-based market is formed and facilitated through some institutions at some stage. In this analysis we have not introduced the complexities of money-based exchange. We have relied on the simplistic interdependence in terms of commodities produced and exchanged (need-based). In this frame, the system repeats itself if there does not occur technological change. The system changes with respect to non-identical command position, derived from changing technology.

II. Consensus on Commodity Production

Production of commodities in an economic system is a reflection of cooperation between (i) people working inside a plant, and (ii) people employed inside a plant and potential workers (job seekers in the working age) outside the plant.

There are owners of labour power and owners of non-labour resources inside a plant. This second category is the owners of material resources and machinery. Any cooperation between these two categories inside a plant is derived from an exercise of uneven but changing bargaining power of these two categories. An immediate reflection of this exercise of power is wage-agreement or agreement on benefits to the respective categories. The conflict between labour reward and non-labour reward is revealed inside a plant, which may be resolved ultimately by selecting technologies of higher order by the owners of non-labour resources. Advanced technologies offer the scope of higher wages corresponding to increased productivity of existing labourers. Higher wages are not dissociated from higher returns on non-labour resources. In absence of crowding in of investment possibilities, it may lead to (i) possible exit of a section of labourers from the existing plants where they are employed, or (ii) raising the burden on the rest of the economy via increasing the size of the unemployed workers or shrinkage of scope for potential labourers outside to be employed in existing plants (Majumder, 2001, p. 92-96). Thus, ultimately the 'required consensus' rotates not only inside the domain of a single plant or all the plants operating in an economy at a particular point of time, but on the possibility of shock absorption by all the people in the economy. We then come to (ii).

If a process of growth and consumption is visible to all, then the benefits and costs have to be shared by all. The people outside the plant at present or beyond the domain of production will have to abide by the norms of a commodity producing society. These norms aim at development of a man to suit the requirements of a commodity producing society.

Development of technology forms an advanced stage of production that leads to a shifting of plants far away from labour-dependence. The application of higher-order technology by the 'new producers' not only ensures long-term benefits but also curtails immediate pressure from owners of labour inside the plant via the offer of high labour rewards. Labourers respond to money wages and hence accept this solution.

It is clear by now that the application of higher order technology-led command differential leads to a situation where a major section of population becomes non-participants in economic activities. How does the system work if there is a strong legal frame to ensure the rights of participants? The implicit conditions are:

- There is an implicit agreement between non-participants (voters in the political system) and the Government that the latter will ensure social security for the former, e.g., in the form of unemployment insurance/allowance etc.

- There is an implicit agreement between participants (voters in the political system) and the Government that the property of the former will be secured and their participation in economic activities will be protected subject to their paying taxes etc. to the Government.

- There is an implicit agreement between non-participants and participants that the latter will provide 'benefits' for the former; if not, the former may apply force (illegal) to extract benefits from the former.

How does the question on consensus come regarding production of commodities in an economy by participants willing (and unobstructed) to participate?

The key lies in command differential derived from technology-differential. One may try to explain command-differential in terms of ownership over natural resources. Such an attempt assumes away explanation of how the right of exclusion is conferred on a few individuals. Let initial commodity production start at a point of time by individuals with equal access to natural resources. With respect to forward moving physical time, some of these individuals will acquire more power (owning and using natural resources) to move ahead relative to others, because of application of superior technology (particularly their superior brainpower developed via learning by doing). If unequal access to natural resources is taken as the starting point then the phenomenon during the time interval on the forward moving time horizon is ignored, with possibilities of wrong implications. Hence, we stress on technology-differential as an explanation of command-differential and this brings the question of selecting commodities by individuals to derive highest attainable command in attainable commodity basket.

Do participants (to the exclusion of non-participants) arrive at a consensus regarding commodity production? Each participant is an optimizer of her/his own goal. Each tries to develop higher order product and technology, thus threatening some participants to face exit in absence of 'at least equal improvement' in acquiring technology. Even if all the participants have the same optimization target with equal access to information and natural resources at the same point of time, 'inter-temporal inter-personal' inequality in forward movement is inevitable. Since there can not be any mechanism in any system, which equalizes 'human brain' in operation, this inequality or command-differential is a natural consequence. Unequal participation can not bring about a permanent consensus. The problem may be more serious since the stake of the non-participants is least in non-cooperation in any system.

III Production, Command, and Development: Some Concluding Comments

Commodity is the wheel that makes man move: movement from the point of production to the point of consumption, via exchange and distribution. The link between initial commodity (collected or transformed) and final (may be intermediates also, depending on the production chain) commodity in the production chain lies in technology. The system works as follows:

Initial technology (applied on nature) — Initial output — Learning by doing — Knowledge — Improved technology — Expansion in production boundary — Development.

Commodity production of a particular type (technology associated) leads to the development of a specific relation between participants, between participants and non-participants, between both on the one hand and with nature on the other. This relation may be both accommodative and non-accommodative. The path of development is derived from the interplay of these dual forces. The non-accommodative relation needs a shock absorber to ensure uninterrupted path of development. This is where the questions related to institutions come, which is beyond the scope of this paper.

References

Chakravarty, S., 1988, 'Development of Development Thinking', Arthavijnana, Vol. XXX, No. 2, June.

Hicks, J.R., 1965, Capital and Growth, Oxford Univ. Press, London.

Hicks, J.R., 1971, The Social Framework, Oxford Univ. Press.

Kerr, P., 1993, 'Adam Smith's Theory of Growth and Technological Change', Contributions to Political Economy, Vol. 12.

Kuznets, S., 1961, Six Lectures on Economic Growth, The Free Press, USA.

Kuznets, S., 1965, Economic Growth and Structure, W.W. Norton And Co., New York.

Majumder, Bhaskar, 2001, 'Technological Progress and Redundancy of Workers: Tasks for Rehabilitation', Labour & Development, Vol. 7, No. 2, Dec.

Stewart, F., 1977, Technology and Underdevelopment, Macmillan.

2

Manpower Mobility in an Era of Globalization: Some Issues

Globalization of production (Gordon, 1988), often described as a process of a 'Decline of Nationalism' (Griffin, 1981), is an event of the recent past. The post-Second World War world has been compartmentalized into a dominant group of industrialized countries, and a subordinate group of non-industrialized or industrializing countries. Globalization is a process of enveloping the latter by the former through application of finance-military-technology power. The industrializing countries of the 1990s have accepted, by choice or by compulsion, market mechanism rather than centralized control for allocation of resources. It is at the same time true that the State in each country now industrialized has been the driving force for transformation of resources to ensure the infrastructure necessary for capitalist industrialization.

We accept a relation of proportionality between the rate of economic growth and the rate of increase in quality-weighted labour force or manpower. In the context of globalization, manpower planning will have dual dimensions, one being planning for man and the other planning for industrialization. In the former, the aim is to ensure a sense of participation for man in production and related activities. This rests on development and hence mobility of man with the aid of knowledge. In the latter, planning for structural adjustment in an industrial society today requires that man is thrown in, and not thrown out, of industrial production activities. Both these dimensions require that the market-determined strategy of manpower mobility is to be supported by, and often preceded by, the generation of job opportunities to ensure the success of globalization for man and for industrialization of the nation state.

Technology, Employment and Manpower Mobility

Less developed countries in general are characterized by immobility of labourers. This is not because that the labourers do not like to be mobile but because they are not informed about 'better' job opportunities elsewhere, whether job opportunities exist at all, or because they are unable, individually and institutionally, to be present elsewhere. Thus when we talk about manpower mobility, we mean 'vertical mobility' and not a horizontal one. The question of capability and opportunity is relevant in the case of vertical mobility. It involves higher wages and better working conditions and/or better establishment/status.

We consider here inter-industrial mobility and rule out dual existence of man. In this context he is not a casual labourer, nor a part-timer. He is a full time permanent employee in a single firm at a time. We consider, in short, inter-industrial vertical mobility of man and exclude the other types (Kerr, 1954).

Labour mobility as such is conditioned at the starting point, by additional job opportunities, and subsequently supported by wage flexibility and wage-differential. With no additional labour absorption in the macro economy, there may occur intra and inter-sectoral reallocation of labour. But in a state of increasing population, it would imply increasing unemployment that may cross the limit of socio-political tolerance. Thus effective labour mobility also requires increasing job opportunities.

Let k denote capital labour ratio or capital per capita,
K physical capital stock,
L labour number (quantity)
Then,

$$k = \frac{K}{L} \rightarrow \quad (1)$$

Taking log in (1) and differentiating with respect to time (t) we get

$$\frac{\dot{L}}{L} = \frac{\dot{K}}{K} - \frac{\dot{k}}{k} \rightarrow \quad (2) \quad \text{Where dot (.) means } \frac{d()}{dt}$$

Equation (2) implies that

Rate of additional labour absorption = Rate of capital accumulation - Rate of capital intensity.

So, labour employment is conditioned by the way capital is used and added.

Let, v denote capital-output ratio,
Q physical volume of output
AP_L average product of labour

$$\text{Thus, } v = \frac{K}{Q} \rightarrow \quad (3)$$

$$\text{or, } v = \frac{K/L}{Q/L} \rightarrow$$

$$\text{or, } v = \frac{k}{AP_L} \rightarrow \quad (4)$$

Taking log in (4) and differentiating with respect to time (t) we get

$$\frac{\dot{v}}{v} = \frac{\dot{k}}{k} - \frac{\dot{AP_L}}{AP_L} \rightarrow \quad (5)$$

or,

$$\frac{\dot{k}}{k} = \frac{\dot{v}}{v} + \frac{\dot{AP_L}}{AP_L} \rightarrow \quad (6)$$

From (3) Similarly,

$$\frac{\dot{K}}{K}=\frac{\dot{Q}}{Q}+\frac{\dot{v}}{v}\rightarrow \qquad (7)$$

From (2) and (6)

$$\frac{\dot{L}}{L}=\frac{\dot{K}}{K}-\frac{\dot{v}}{v}-\frac{A\dot{P}_L}{AP_L}\rightarrow \qquad (8)$$

From (2) and (7)

$$\frac{\dot{L}}{L}=\frac{\dot{Q}}{Q}+\frac{\dot{v}}{v}-\frac{\dot{k}}{k}\rightarrow \qquad (9)$$

From (8) and (9)

$$\frac{\dot{K}}{K}=2\frac{\dot{v}}{v}+\frac{\dot{Q}}{Q}+\frac{A\dot{P}_L}{AP_L}-\frac{\dot{k}}{k}\rightarrow \qquad (10)$$

From (2) and (10)

$$\frac{\dot{L}}{L}=2\frac{\dot{v}}{v}+\frac{\dot{Q}}{Q}+\frac{A\dot{P}_L}{AP_L}-2\frac{\dot{k}}{k}\rightarrow \qquad (11)$$

Obviously R.H.S. in (11) shows non-exhaustive technological conditions of labour employment. The forces that favour labour employment are productivity of labour and growth of output, inverse of productivity of capital and inverse of capital-intensity.

We have considered the technological options for additional labour absorption, and hence labour mobility. We use an example to explain its rationality.

Let there be two firms in two industries producing two different products paying different wage rates. Two persons, a and b, (or two groups of persons) are employed in firms A and B respectively. We assume no exit of firms and persons. We assume existence of job-seekers outside at the prevailing wage rate, wherever it is.

	Example		
(1)	Firms	A B	
(2)	Existing Manpower	a b	
(3)	Mobility cases		Reaction (implication)
	I. No Entry	(i) 0 b + a	Exit of A
		(ii) a + b 0	Exit of B
		(iii) c b + a	Person c is a new entry in A, while a moves to B.
		(iv) a + c b	Person c is a new entry in A, with no mobility
	II. Positive Entry	(v) a + b c	Person c is a new entry in B, while b moves to A.
		(vi) b + c a	Person c is a new entry in A, while b moves to A and a to B.
		(vii) a b + c	Person c is a new entry in B, with no mobility.
		(viii) b a + c	Person c is a new entry in B, while a moves to B and b moves to A.

Here (i) and (ii) are ruled out by assumption; (iv) and (vii) show only new absorption and no mobility. The cases, (iii), (v) and (viii) indicate labour mobility in a situation of additional labour absorption.

One firm does not employ only one person, but a hierarchy of persons, interdependent in production of commodities. Even then if a person moves to another job, his position is to be filled in by absorption of another person, on the assumption that the initial appointment was rational and on the assumption of continuation of complementarities between other inputs and manpower. Thus the question of labour mobility is to be seen in a frame of labour absorption.

It is rational for a firm to discourage the exit of skilled labourers, thereby obstructing mobility. But paradoxically, the same firm encourages the entry of skilled labourers from other firms, thereby inviting mobility. Every firm thus has a dual face on the question of labour mobility. From the viewpoint of all the firms taken together, it is a zero-sum game, the question being initial allocation of manpower and its subsequent reallocation. It becomes a non-zero-sum game when the implications of altered allocation are considered. Thus the movement of a national economy requires manpower mobility.

It is by now generally accepted that the global development gap does not lie merely in the difference in the technological levels. In particular, the demand for high level manpower in developed countries arises not from the current technological structure but from the concern for improving the technology. Thus, the demand for such manpower arises from a concern for raising the output per man, i.e., the productivity of labour (Dasgupta, 1991, p. 64-65).

Not only did the governments in developing countries for non-economic reasons commit to raising labour employment often at the cost of surrendering labour productivity, but the governments in developed countries also at some historical juncture adopted similar types of policies, e.g., the Employment Act of 1946 in U.S. economy (Magnum, 1967, p. 11) when in fact, in the context of choosing appropriate technologies, an apparent conflict between labour employment and labour productivity disappears.

'Repetitive import of technologies' in countries like India is seen as an easy substitute often rationalized as a techno-economic perfectionist attitude of the Government, for generation of socially appropriate technologies, technologies which would have selected in, and not selected out, labourers with non-falling productivity

(Mascarenhas, 1982). There was no internal compulsion for the choice of appropriate technology in a 'protected regime' for firms characterized by monopolistic and oligopolistic features (Majumder, 1990).

The indifference towards raising labour productivity by the Governments in such countries breaks down in the context of globalization. While this globalization is likely to lead to increasing demand for skilled labourers because of increasing weightage of research-intensive products and projects, it also makes some employed labourers obsolete and some potential labourers unemployable. The relevance of manpower planning comes here.

Manpower Mobility in terms of Wage-differential

The New International Economic Order has brought about a compelling necessity to concentrate on the problems related to the supply and mobility of labour, the compulsion reflected in the exit of labourers and often the exit of the product/firm itself (Streeten, 1982). The problem is not a new one, however. On the theoretical plane, "Since 1940 ... considerable interest in the movement of labour within a local labour market ... grew out of a dissatisfaction with the traditional assumption of the economic theory about the movement of workers from one job to another in response to differences in wage rates" (Myers, 1954, p. 68). Functionally, irrespective of globalization, there occurred 'Brain Drain' from the LDCs even in a situation of internal shortage of supervisors and technicians at all levels of skill (ILO, 1966).

While the international wage-differential dominantly drains manpower out from an LDC, it is not always the case for vertical labour mobility inside the country. Given the industrial order, the workers move from one industry to another, if they move at all, without requiring any remarkable wage-differential, e.g., "a higher wage might be necessary to attract workers to an expanding industry, or it might simply reflect the fact that the union concerned has taken advantage of the increasing level of demand to negotiate a higher wage, even though enough workers would in fact have been forthcoming at the old wage in response to offers of employment" (Reddaway, 1968, p. 194-195). In countries like India, often the exercise of bargaining power for wage is productivity-neutral and psephology-determined (Bardhan, 1984). This wage rate is fixed in advance generally for not less than five years whatever the productivity conditions are. This is no exception for LDCs in advanced countries, e.g. in the USA in the 1960s it was the case (Lester, 1967). It is, however, likely that some research-intensive firms in need of technologists may be forced temporarily to shoot up the wage rate, when in particular demand for such skilled labour exceeds its supply, it takes much time to re-educate and re-train mass of labourers, or face the consequences of 'brain drain' (OECD, 1965).

Generally the flexibility in wage rate is product-specific and skill-specific. If the products are research-intensive, the wage-rate is expected to be high to attract 'brain' or to obstruct 'brain drain'. Wage rate is often raised for ranks above some level to exclude unskilled labourers. Also, in a setting of wage-ranked hierarchy of industries, an industry in the rank of a high wage may feel it less necessary to raise the wage rate relative to industries in the low wage category to attract labourers. The introduction of globalization by the leaders of the globe may complicate the situation, e.g., imposition of artificial wage-structure for a few firms selected by bias.

In spite of its many shortcomings, the wage rate is often used as an instrument for allocating labour among alternative production areas. Since the wage rate is quantifiable, the labourers foresee this rate and make their expectations about this rate. Ceteris paribus, the labourers prefer a higher-wage job to a lower-wage one. The question is who is going to honour the choice of the potential labourers even when this preference pattern in known to the employers/Trade Unions/Government and which is backed by the capability of the labourers? The solution is constrained further by the existence of an unlimited supply of labourers in such countries.

The fact is that a labourer joins a job often independent of his own choice or in conditions of ignorance (Rottenberg, 1968). What the labourer can choose is to change the job after acquiring the power to be mobile. For vertical mobility, the summation of benefits must be higher for the labourer willing to move. However, workers' access to information on wage and non-wage terms of employment in other companies is insignificant (Reynolds, 1951, p. 213). In fact, if we assume that the labourers are aware of the existence of the wage-differential in similar jobs, then it makes sense that, ceteris paribus, the labour mobility will be a direct function of wage-differential. If the labour market is perfect, the labourers are rational optimizers. However, in practice, the labour market is heterogeneous and highly imperfect (Banerjee, 1988). In this situation labour mobility, if any, is wage-insensitive or there come non-wage factors and forces to cause immobility of labourers.

Rigidity and Flexibility in Labour Market

Mixed capitalist economies like India subject to 'State Control' via economic planning and public enterprises are characterized by an industrial sector dual in character. In most cases, the establishments develop an 'internally closed system', allowing entry into the establishments at the lowest level or providing limited entry points. Most positions in the establishments are filled through internal promotions, offering little opportunities for competition. This is peculiar not only to LDCs. In advanced countries, e.g., in the U.K. "all members of bureaucracy stand to gain from further bureaucratic growth, since this tends to accentuate personal incomes, promotion prospects, power, patronage and sometimes public respect. Rent-seeking typically is more effective in the public than in the private sector because the public sector is more monopolistic, tends to be less efficient, and information flows more easily are distorted" (Rowley, 1980, p. 44). Again from the U.K. experience it is revealed that not only the employers and bureaucrats but also the trade unions may obstruct the entry of the outsiders (Mackay, 1971, p. 300). Thus there come institutional-cum-administrative barriers to entry and mobility of labourers, more so when the public sector dominates.

In LDCs in particular, non-contractual, productivity-neutral labour employment based on provision for time-scale salary and seniority based uplift leads to higher designation and probably higher degradation. Often labourers do not like to move from low wage certainty to high-wage uncertainty. As labour mobility requires execution of additional responsibilities by establishments, it is generally discouraged. All these lead to a situation where the small well-knit organized sector becomes immune from market forces. The private sector units also, through acquisition of license, become instruments of the government, and cease to behave as competitive economic units, gaining more from collusion, and less from competitive entrepreneurship.

Thus the rigidity experienced from the increased domination of public sector may continue to prevail even if the private sector gains domination via reducing 'State Control' disinvestment in public enterprises and economic liberalization (GOI, 1991, p. 4). The rigidity in labour market thus is sector-neutral and plan-neutral. It is basically rooted in the socio-political structure of the society.

Often inter-industrial vertical mobility of labour is constrained by imposition of political (in) discipline, e.g., manpower absorption in enterprises, both public and private, above some wage category is determined by 'political quota'; family-centered business, where not only in tiny, informal and unorganized sector but also in organized industrial production areas, there is limited entry for 'outsiders' and often jobs in the high wage occupations are reserved for persons in, or connected with, the affluent society; colonial heritage, where people educated abroad are preferred to people educated inside; non-innovative or stereotype jobs, where internal manpower is preferred to external ones.

Some segmented entry and obstructions may be there in such an imperfect, often externally open and internally closed labour market. For example, for budding technologists and managers, often there is provision for 'campus recruitment' by established firms. Here the rate of reward per rupee spent on education is high relative to the social average expenditure on education. If this rate falls short of the expectation of the individual by international comparison, there may occur brain drain. Often the nature of entry into the job market is 'time-tied', making manpower mobility non-operational for the stipulated period. Often highly qualified persons are obstructed from entering middle-level and below that rank job lest they leave the job at the very first opportunity because of their positive opportunity cost. Potential vertical mobility becomes a disqualification for such persons. Some types of entry may be delinked from any guarantee of jobs, e.g. Apprenticeship Schemes.

The rigidity and flexibility of the heterogeneous labour market in countries like India thus are linked with such factors, often excluded as 'residuals'. They, however, may affect the market more than the wage rate, its flexibility and differential.

Necessity of Manpower Planning

Whatever be the constraints and peculiarities of labour mobility in LDCs like India, it is a universal fact that knowledge is space-neutral and hence application of knowledge in production, or technology, is a global aspect.

In the context of globalization then, the process of scientific and technological collaboration between countries has to be based on an 'Open door, Open window' model as opposed to a 'Closed door, Open window' model (Dandekar, 1968, p. 232). Science has to move freely for the generation of scientific outlook in man and the formation of a birth-neutral society. Manpower planning in this context has to work both as a transmitter and an antenna, the former transmitting knowledge (may be via the outflow of skilled personnel), the latter receiving knowledge (via the inflow of skilled personnel and relevant technology, relevance determined by initial condition and future choice). While the former is a moral compulsion for the State to ensure international mobility to the individual optimizer, the latter is an economic compulsion. In fact, inflow of information is the power of the State.

By implication, globalization is not an end or even a decline of nationalism. One merely moves beyond the national orbit. Occasionally we talk about initial conditions posing problems in the sense of imposing constraints on labour mobility in particular and on the process of development of the later-starters in general. Apparently these initial conditions manifest themselves in the lack of power to generate and absorb technologies for revolutionization of a society. The real roots for countries like India lie in ignorance, illiteracy and rampant miseducation of the mass, often anti-life outlook, alienation of the educated elite from the mass and often more vulnerability of this section alienated from the mainstream in the shape of acute dependence on and collusion with foreign rulers and powers (Myrdal, 1982).

Effectively it would mean that manpower planning has to take care of ensuring education and training for the workforce inside the job, initiating programmes in the sphere of production for ensuring the flow of required machinery and equipment, initiating educational planning for people out of jobs to make them employable and job guarantee for the employable inside and outside the nation state. Since production is a reflection of social cooperation, reflected in the plant between labourers of varying skills, in the consensus between people inside the plant and people outside, the state has to adopt two mutually supporting steps, one being product-cum-technology planning and the other manpower planning. The second type of planning is vital for the development of 'consensus' of the agents of change inside the nation to accept the first type. Education is the root of power, the root of local and global power-differential. Educational planning is the instrument of manpower planning for the nation and that is non-ending nationalism.

References

Banerjee, N. (1988), 'The Unorganized Sector and the Planner', in A.K. Bagchi (Ed), 'Economy, Society and Polity, Essays in the Political Economy of Indian Planning', OUP.

Bardhan, P. (1984), The Political Economy of Development in India, OUP.

Dandakar, A.K. (1968), 'India' in Adams, in Walter (Ed.) 'The Brain Drain', The Macmillan Company, New York.

Dasgupta, A.K. (1991), 'Foundation and Structure of Real Resource Based Planning for Economic Growth, Seminar (Alternative Manpower Planning Structure), Paper, IAMR, New Delhi, January 6-7.

Government of India, (1991), 'India's New Economic Policies', Ministry of External Affairs, New Delhi.

Gorden, David, M. (1988) 'The Global Economy: New Edifice or Crumbling Foundations?', New Left Review, No. 168, March-April.

Griffin, Keith, (1981), 'Economic Development in a Changing World', World Development, Vol. 9, No. 3, March

International Labour Office (ILO), (1966), Report of the Director General, Part I, International Labour Conference, 50th Session, Geneva.

Kerr, Clark (1954) 'The Balkanization of labour Markets', in Bakke, E.W. et al, 'Labour Mobility and Economic Opportunity', The Technology Press, New York.

Lester, Richard A. (1967), 'The Role of Organized Labour', in Gordon, Robert A. (Ed.), 'Toward a Manpower Policy', John Wiley & Sons, Inc.

Mackay, D.I. & Others (1971), 'Labour Markets under Different Employment Conditions', George Allen & Unwin Ltd., London, 1971.

Magnum, Garth L. (1967), The National Programme, in Gordon, Robert A, Op. Cit.

Majumder, Bhaskar, (1990), 'Import Substituting Industrialization Strategy in Indian Economy: An Evaluation', The Indian Journal of Economics, Vol. XXXI, Part I, Oct.

Mascarenhas, R.C. (1982), 'Technology, Trade and Development: India's HMT Company', A West View Replica Ed., West View Press, Colorado.

Myers, Charles A (1954), 'Labour Mobility in Two countries', in E. W. Bakke et al, Op Cit.

Myrdal,Gunnar (1982) 'Asian Drama: An Enquiry into the Poverty of Nations', Vol. III, Kalyani Publishers, New Delhi.

Organization for Economic Cooperation and Development, (OECD) (1965), 'Wages and Labour Mobility', Paris, July.

Reddaway, W.B. (1968), 'Wage Flexibility and the Distribution of Labour', in McCormic B.J. & Smith, Owen E. (E.D.), 'The labour Market, Selected Reading', Penguin Books.

Rottenberg, S., (1968), 'On Choice in labour Markets', in McCormic & Smith (Ed.) Op. cit.

Reynolds, Lloyds G., (1951), 'The Structure of Labour Markets', Harper & Brothers, New York.

Rowlery, Charles, (1980), 'Industrial Policy in the Mixed Economy', in Lord Roll of Ipsden (Ed), 'The Mixed Economy', Macmillan Press, London.

Streeten, Paul, (1982), 'Approaches to a New International Economic Order', World Development, Vol. 10, No.1.

3

Globalized Indian Economy: Some Reflections on Workers' Mobility

The post-Second World War world is globalized in a bipolar world and the post-Cold War world is globalized in a unipolar world. In keeping with the macro economic stabilization and structural adjustment policies (SAP) advocated by the institutions like the World Bank (WB) and the International Monetary Fund (IMF), the Government of India declared its New Economic Policy (NEP) in 1991. The NEP, 1991 aimed at ensuring 'much free play of market forces' (GOI, 1991, p. 5). The non-enforcement of 'local content requirement' as well as the non-enforcement of 'indigenisation in manufacturing' as declared in the NEP 1991, will have implications on the scope for labour requirements at home in future (GOI, 1991, p. 3).

The NEP was supposed to have implications for labour vis-à-vis capital. While capital is directly owned or controlled by the capitalists or the managers of capital, labour of the potential workers is not directly controlled as such. Families are the immediate suppliers of labour while they are the remote suppliers of capital.

Capital comes to its controllers (firms) through financial institutions that collect savings (money) from the families. However, the participation of the workers comes through the existence and operations of firms. These firms control both capital and labour, and coordinate between these in the sphere of production. The individual as a labourer sells her labour power where the firm, as the owner or controller of capital, agrees to buy it. This, at the same time, shows the control of capital over labour. This control of labour by capital gets more power when the technology assists capital in deciding the existence and exit of labour.

The integration of the national economies aims at non-discrimination between home and foreign firms. The countries like India generally depend for technologies and investment on foreign firms. 'Non-discrimination' in the globalization agenda means offering 'home treatment' for foreign firms in the host country where the home firm is located. A cordial relationship between foreign firms and home firms on the home soil means also rationalization of firms through a number of means. These means may include technological upgradation, shifting control of capital from the public to the private, and downsizing of workers. For example, following the NEP, 1991 for a specified list of high technology and high investment priority industries, (home) firms will receive automatic approval to make any foreign technology agreements within certain guidelines (GOI, 1991, p. 4). These may, in turn, lead to adoption of high-technology-led eviction of workers calculated to be crowded in a particular firm. This in parallel may lead to increasing informalization of labour force and decline of labour as a class in two ways, one through decline of trade unionism, and the other through decline in real wage rate. Both these ways are interlinked; the latter follows the reducing bargaining power of labour vis-à-vis capital.

This paper is structured into four sections. In section I, we discuss labour-related conditions for globalization by production relocation. In section II, we focus on work opportunities and weakening of labour as a class. In section III, we consider issues on labour mobility and workers' exodus. Finally, in section IV, we offer concluding comments.

(I) Labour as a Necessary Condition for Relocation of Production

We take the following two assumptions for the global operations of firms within the capitalist production system as a pre-condition to examine labour as a necessary condition:

(i) for any firm, profit maximization, or its proxy, sales maximization, subject to minimum profit constraint, as the objective function.

(ii) for all firms taken together, non-redundancy of labour from demand side even as a consequence of technological improvement.

Location of a plant by a firm is conditional upon the existence of a labour force ready to sell labour-power at any positive price that is acceptable to the owner of non-labour resources. We have in mind the existence of 'cheap labour' in the TWCs. The TNCs, originating in the DMEs, deal with trade unions and consumer organizations and environmentalists that often oppose their interests at home. These institutions are much weaker in the TWCs. Hence, the TNCs often prefer the TWCs as the probable locations of the TNCs.

The 'cheap labour' argument stands on some of the following factors:

- Unlimited supply of labourers

- Positive and sizeable unemployment, maintained below the level that may bring about political risk, but at the rate that is necessary for the firm to expect downward pressure on the wage rate;

- Keeping an informal sector for absorption of labourers in the formal sector who face exit and for the job-seekers in general;

- Socio-political apathy towards the unemployed;
- Government-centered society or social groups;
- Non-existence of labour legislation;
- Weak labour legislation;
- Weak trade unions or trade unions working at cross purposes
- Anti-labour attitude of government where the plant is to be located;
- Political stability, even in a situation of anti-labour policy camouflaged by government;
- Authoritarian political regime;
- Oppressive/coercive government, e.g., Military Government;
- Absence of State protection of labourers, e.g. absence of Unemployment Insurance/Allowance;
- Absence of Minimum Wage Act and/or non-functioning or irrelevant act;
- Ignorance of the population in the working age about labour market.

Apart from the TNC-led use of labourers of the host country within its own geographic boundary, the DMEs also use the Third World as a source of skilled labour to be brought to their economies. While the TWCs are the hosts of the DMEs for capital and technology, the DMEs are the hosts of the TWCs by being buyers of labour-power through direct entry of Third World labourers into the DMEs. These labourers get wages higher than what they would have received in their home countries, but much less than what the host governments and firms would have had to give had they employed the home workers. The process of generation of surplus in production, hence, gets accentuated for the host DMEs. This process may also be called 'inverse technology transfer'.

(II) Work Opportunities and Weakening of Labour as a Class

In localized economies of most of the underdeveloped countries, family is the unit for decision-making, and not the individual. The family as a whole provides income security. It is a collective economy where family priorities come ahead of the individual's self-priorities. The family is the economic unit, not the individual. The revealed choices of an individual are really the reflections of simultaneous decisions of all members in the family that attempt to optimize family welfare, with the gains and losses of all the members of the family entering into the decision. Decisions on migration are no exceptions (Feam, 1981, p. 236). In countries in Asia and Africa, family as a unit remains central for employment and migration (ILO, 2000, p. 24). Many of these local economies may not also show uniform pattern of work opportunities and conditions of workers. The region like Kerala in India shows more mobility of workers relative to many other regions within the same national economy. The region like Bihar shows more shifts of workers, often poverty-driven, to adjoining region like West Bengal and also to remote region like Punjab, relative to workers in Uttar Pradesh. Even within Uttar Pradesh one finds regional variations in workers mobility, not necessarily by consequence but by initial conditions. For example, a recent study has recorded near absence of 'out migration' from the settled localities in the district of Muzaffarnagar in the extreme west UP as well as from the district Deoria in the extreme east UP. The initial conditions of the same consequence, however, are different. While in west UP workers 'in migrate' there being scope for labour absorption, out migration remains absent for east UP because of non-information or unawareness of the available workers in addition to non-immigration in east UP (Majumder, 2005). The compulsions, opportunities and willingness to go beyond the small boundary of expected available jobs make a section of workers more mobile relative to others.

Generally the local economic units show informal nature of employment. In general, the written, formal contracts governing the economic exchanges between buyers and sellers and between employers and employees are absent because of pre-capitalistic institutional arrangements. Informal units comprise small enterprises with hired workers, while household "enterprises" use mostly family labour. Production processes involve relatively high levels of working capital as against fixed capital, which in turn reflects the relatively low level of technology and skills involved. While the small enterprises could well be involved in continuous production processes, most units engage in batch production methods and are seasonal in nature (ILO 1998-99, p. 167). The working inability of the workers in plants in the technologically changing circumstances aggravates the situation, if they are absorbed in the formal sector. In India, for example, a large proportion of the labour force is illiterate. A major part of industry with the exception of a few multinationals and a few large-scale employers depends upon informal channels to recruit and train its workforce. While the informal apprenticeship system ('ustaad-shagrid', that is, teacher-assistant) has many elements which make it attractive in terms of cheap on-the-job training, the cost in terms of quality and productivity may be high (ILO, 1998-99, p. 126).

For the workers settled in the economically backward regions, the employment pattern remains complex. A recent study has revealed that calculation of man days may not carry much meaning if the plan of employment is to encompass as many workers as possible. For example, the study found the same number of workers used in a number of works like earth digging and filling, rural link road construction, construction of drains, desilting of canals etc. during the off-agricultural season in many regions in UP (Majumder, 2004). While a worker is engaged in a number of works at the local level, which is not to be confused with diversification of jobs, most of the workers remain jobless for a significant period of any year. The study found that for UP, during the off-agriculture season, employment for a period on average only 10 – 12 days per year per adult individual was available in the working age under Food for work scheme. This employment by number of days, in addition to being insignificant, may conceal the opportunity for a few individuals in multiple jobs. A high number of man days generated thus may not necessarily encompass high number of workers actually employed.

(III) Labour Mobility or Workers' Exodus?

Any question related to labour employment globally carries operational meaning when the facts revealed in the developed capitalist countries (OECD) are juxtaposed vis-à-vis the often concealed facts (non-recorded/non-disseminated) in the TWCs. Let us look at labour force participation rates for India and for regions (Table 1).

Table 1. Labour Force Participation Rates at Age 15-64, 1980-2000

Region/Country	*1980*	*1995*	*2000*
World	72.6	73.0	73.3
More developed regions	71.4	72.7	73.1
Less developed regions	73.1	73.4	73.4
Least developed regions	78.7	77.2	76.8
India	68.9	66.4	66.6

Source : ILO, 2000, World Labour Report, pp. 267-268.

Prima facie, the data for all the countries based on regional average show similar rates of labour force participation. India conforms to this pattern. The data show nothing more than the size of population in the specified age brackets that deem to be economically active. What the data fail to capture is the very nature of employment. In the less developed regions comprising countries in Asia (excluding Japan), Africa and Latin America, most of the people remain dependent on land (agriculture). The social structure in most of these countries being accommodative and the economic structure being pre-capitalistic, the people in the working age remain less mobile. Underemployment or low-productivity based employment is the corollary.

Ground Reality

Most of the population in both working and non-working age (children and aged) in the Third World countries depends on agriculture and land-based activities for mere survival. The questions related to the pattern of labour employment like part-time, casual etc. are meaningless in most of these cases. In a large country like India by size of total population, and hence population in the working age, this means absence of any choice for the individuals in families other than being dependent on land. All the Census data since 1961 on percentage distribution of the workforce in rural India have shown hardly any change for both male and female. For male workers the percentage varies between 76.0 and 81.0 per cent and for female workers it varies between 84.0 and 88.0 per cent. The National Sample Survey (NSS), which has followed comparable definitions on employment and unemployment, shows a similar trend (NIRD, 1999, p. 55-56). The consequences are obvious. Without technological change it means reducing land-cum-labour productivity, while with technological change it means displacement of a section of the initial 'wage workers'. The second one also may imply surrender (leasing-out) of small plots of land to the big landholders, because technology happens to be too costly for the very small farmer, by size of land and capacity to input-use, to adopt.

The problems become more interesting when it is not a single work for many of the workers. While this may lead to the problem of identification of the worker, it also leads to complicate the calculations that we discussed so far. While land productivity can be measured by physical volume of output, worker productivity may be made fuzzy by price manipulations. In fact, the whole of income (productivity) of workers in the service sector is a reflection of this price manipulation. In case of multiple jobs, often by selection by distress as opposed to diversification, income-criteria are thought of to identify the worker. Thus, if individual X is self-employed in agricultural work for eight months a year and earns Rs. 20,000 in total, while she works in a mill for four months as casual worker and earns Rs. 20,001, she will be called a casual (wage) worker (freeter). If X works for six months a year in agriculture and earns Rs. 15,000 while in a mill she works for six months to earn Rs. 30,000 she will, for sure, be called a casual (wage) worker. In the former case, we need to take care of the time spent in agricultural activities and in both the cases we need to take care of the attachment of the individual to land. The point is whatever temporary job the individual selects, she is land-based for not only earning but also for stable living. Hence, it will be more rational to identify the worker as agricultural worker, whether she is self-employed in agriculture or employed by others. In case of self-employment, this argument will invite fewer debates, while in case of hired employment it will invite debate.

The question on mobility of factors of production in conventional economic analysis treats all factors as similar. Thus, mobility of labour (measured perhaps by labour hour) is considered in a production function in the same way as mobility of capital. However, neither as a cause nor as a consequence are they the same.

Capital is mobile because of decisions by workers (these workers may be called the managers in a hierarchic frame of production). Even the electronic speed of capital is because of click of push button of workers engaged with the system of electronic communication. The knowledge of workers can move at an electronic speed but not the worker herself. The way the workers get affected by the utilization of capital and other factors are obviously not the same as the way capital and other inanimate factors are affected. The ways by which labour, capital and other factors are affected are linked with many factors like market size, technology, access to market (trade) etc. Many of these determining factors are also linked with the workers decisions at multi levels and layers.

The mobility that is generally discussed in literature stands on inter-industrial mobility. Generally, it rules out dual existence of man. The individual as an economic agent is not assumed to be a casual (part-time) worker, nor does she share jobs in exchange of income of any type seasonally/occasionally. She is assumed not to be in distress to sell anything that she may be collecting from common resources. She is assumed to have saleable labour (labour power as a commodity) which she readily finds a buyer to buy. This shows a very limited frame for analyzing workers' (often potentially existing) economic existence and mobility.

The industrially less developed countries in general are characterized by immobility of workers. This is not because of the unwillingness of the workers to be mobile but because they are not informed about 'better' job opportunities elsewhere. Worker's mobility is linked with a 'better' job where the worker is not compelled to accept any job anywhere in a situation of 'displacement' or distress of the worker and her family. We have in mind the population in an underdeveloped region/economy in the working age and talk about the alternative phrases like 'mobility', 'migration', 'displacement', 'shift', 'eviction', etc. Even when jobs of any type are available and known to the worker, she may not be in a position to be present everywhere because of initial cost involved, like travel cost and costs for many other necessities for living. The term 'mobility' implicitly implies vertical movement. It involves higher wages and better working conditions and/or better establishment/status. Both capability of the individual and job opportunity are relevant for such mobility.

Labour mobility, thus, is conditioned at the starting point by additional job opportunities and subsequently by wage flexibility and wage-differential. For the national economy inter-regional and inter-industry movement may not necessarily show additional job opportunities for additional workers. It may show reallocation of same labour (by labour hour and by same number of individuals). Thus, meaningful labour mobility requires increasing job opportunities. The law of average may have a tendency to show that labour market in a national economy comes to a balance by equality of demand and supply due to free movement of labour. The reality is that for many of the land-dependent production regions of economies, workers movement is 'direction-less'. The workers are often drawn into the second locality from the first one because the former shows work opportunities for the short period for which there remain no work opportunities in the first locality. This movement for support of family income, whether or not the worker moves alone or with the family, occurs under compulsions. Hence, it should be called displacement as opposed to mobility, of the available workers.

A worker joins a job generally independent of her own choice or in conditions of ignorance (Rottenberg, '968). We are talking about the sphere of production where production is delinked from land and dependent more on invisible coordination of capital, technology and labour. For the organized sector with opportunities to earn stable income, the worker initially at the low age may think of herself more as an individual, and less as a member attached to a family, that enables her to go to join a job offered anywhere. With rising productivity in the initial job the individual attains the capability to choose another job. In an information-friendly environment, the worker may change the initial job by selecting a new one. In a forward moving time sequence the individual assumes new (family) responsibilities by marital status. The worker calculates a trade off between benefits that the new job will provide her and the costs that she will have to incur. These costs are not always visible and not always monetary. However, the workers access to information on wage and non-wage terms of employment in other jobs may not be perfect (Reynolds 1951, p. 231). It also may be that the worker's choice and mobility are responsive to more non-wage factors and forces than the wage-differential if the latter is really known. These non-wage factors are the accommodation of the worker's family, the education of the children in a new region with all new linguistic-cultural implications. The mobility of the worker, thus, is sharply different from the supply-side behaviour of labour mobility that corresponds to technological conditions that include productivity of labour and capital, rate of growth of output, capital intensity etc. (Majumder, 1995, p. 99).

On the assumption that the initial absorption of workers in a particular plant was rational, it will be rational for a firm to discourage the exit of skilled workers. There is, thus, internal obstruction for worker's mobility. This obstruction is not always visible. The same firm, however, encourages the entry of workers who have proved themselves skilled in other plants, thereby inviting mobility. No firm employs just one person. It is a production system based on cooperation of workers at multiple layers of skill. The plant-specific production, thus, shows interdependence of the workers employed. The prevailing technology does not throw workers out, but the improving technology shows the path of eviction of a section of workers. This is because of the inter-temporal and relative obsolescence of a section of workers employed earlier. If it is not in-house technological improvement executed internally, the firm will have to get it from outside to remain competitive in the market, thereby showing rationalization of the firm. If the firm can foresee obsolescence of employed workers vis-à-vis advanced new technology, it may be interested in re-educating and training of workers. This happens when eviction of workers remains a remote choice. Training of workers by job rotation inside a plant or in an inter-firm level shows shift of workers, and not necessarily mobility by promotion.

The tying and eviction of workers depend on where the workers are initially employed. In traditional land-based activities, one may find tied/bonded workers. In case of land tenure one may find easy eviction of workers. The eviction of settled people from the land they had been cultivating may show subsequent displacement. The project-specific displacement, for example, in case of construction of roads, dams, etc. may lead to displacement of workers from settled localities affected by these infrastructural initiatives. This displacement is independent of the choice of the people in the working age along with their families. These workers may seek jobs anywhere in the national economy, or, even outside the national boundary. The people in the working age may shift to the neighbouring country, country to be settled by determination of state power and independent of the affected people, because of war, partition, etc. and seek jobs in the new settled region. These people are often called refugees or people who sought asylum. Engagement in a number of jobs does not always show stability by reduced vulnerability in 'one job', but may show vulnerability of the worker herself when the single initial job is not much dependable. This dependability is subject to the existing market condition and hence the return that the job offers throughout the year and over years.

The workers themselves may show inner-antagonism in an inter-firm frame so far as labour of one is thought to be substitutable for the other. This may obstruct worker's mobility. Often inter-firm mobility of workers may be obstructed by political influence, for example, absorption of workers in both public and private enterprises above some wage level may be determined by 'political quota'. Mobility may also be obstructed by family-centered business where not only in tiny, informal and unorganized sector but also in organized production areas there is limited entry for 'outsiders' and often jobs in the high-wage occupations may be reserved for persons already in, or connected with, the affluent society. Colonial heritage, where people educated in western countries are preferred to people educated inside, may be a 'match-fixer'. Mobility of workers may also be constrained by non-innovative or stereotype jobs, where internal workers 'do the job'. Often the entry of individuals into the job market is 'time-tied', making workers mobility non-operational for a stipulated period. Often highly qualified persons are obstructed from entering into middle-level and below those rank jobs lest they leave the job at the very first opportunity because of their positive opportunity cost. Potential vertical mobility becomes a disqualification for such persons. Some type of entry may be delinked from any guarantee of jobs, for example, Apprenticeship Schemes.

Some segmented entry and obstructions may occur in such an imperfect labour market, for example, for budding technologists and managers often there is provision for 'campus recruitment' by established firms. This also depends on the credibility of the institution where these technologists and managers are budding. In these institutions the per capita expenditure on education, either state-financed or private-financed, is much more than the social average expenditure on education per capita. The rate of return on education is also much higher for the persons coming out successfully from these institutions relative to the institutions that provide general skill. In a globalized economy with easy movement of skilled workers across countries, there occurs drain of these technologists if the rate-differential is thought inadequate to stay in the 'home job' State-financed formation of manpower, thus, adds to the power of the countries outside the 'home country'.

(IV) Concluding Comments

The selection of a region like India for relocation of production by TNCs thus gets concentrated in a narrow frame outside the accommodation-eviction net of the large informal sector. The reality may be more complex than what we have discussed so far. For example, the labour contractors and hence the workers that we think outside the frame of TNCs-led relocation of production possibility boundary may also be accommodated by sub-contracting etc.

The workers identity as wage earners and their mobility depend on a number of factors that we discussed in the frame of a national economy. The analysis becomes more complex if it is extended to consideration of mobility of workers settled in TWCs like India and abroad.

The majority of the workers in the economies of the TWCs is land-based and locally confined other than when they are drawn to a different region under survival compulsions. We discussed in a frame of work opportunities, the technological-institutional implications of workers existence in an economy like India that remains land-based. The recorded percentages of employment and unemployment in such economies will be disturbed if technological advancement is applied on land. This may lead to immediate displacement of a section of workers from land. This will convert underemployment to unemployment. If this displacement is obstructed for socio-political reasons, the consequence may be trapping the increasing population, with probably static percentage of rising total population, to perpetual poverty. Only repenting over the hypothetical phenomenon of underemployment or disguised employment in agriculture will lead to prolonging backwardness. A strong step towards exposing the problem, however, requires planning for rehabilitation of workers on jobs that are based on and consistent with the knowledge base of these workers. Development of agriculture-related activities on an industrial basis, and development of local resource-based rural industries, and public works for both workers' absorption-cum-creation of productive assets are the routes by which this population can be productively employed. The catalyst for these has to be the state. It remains to be seen how the state reacts vis-à-vis forces of integration of the national economy in the global order.

References

Fearn, Robert M., (1981), *Labour Economies: The Emerging Synthesis*, Winthrop Pub. Cambridge.

GOI, Ministry of External Affairs, (1991), *India's New Economic Policies*, New Delhi.

ILO, 1998-99, *World Employment Report*, Geneva.

ILO, 2000, *World Labour Report*, Geneva.

Majumder, Bhaskar, (1995), 'Manpower Mobility in an Era of Globalization: Some Issues', *Productivity*, Vol. 36, No. 1, April-June.

————, (2004), 'Sampoorna Grameen Rozgar Yojana (Food for Work Component), Efficacy and Effectiveness', Report submitted to Planning Commission, GOI.

————, (2005), 'Rural Housing and Living Conditions of People Settled in Rural Uttar Pradesh- A Study', Report submitted to Planning Commission, GOI.

National Institute of Rural Development (NIRD), 1999, India, Rural Development Report, Hyderabad.

Reynolds, Lloyeds, (1951), *The Structure of Labour Markets*, Harper & Brothers, New York.

Rottenberg, (1968), "On Choice in Labour Markets", in McCormic, B. J. and Smith, Owen, E (Ed), *the Labour Market, Selected Readings*, Penguin Books.

4

Informalization of Global Labour and Survival of Local Workers

The post-Second World War is globalized in a bipolar world and the post-Cold War world is globalized in a unipolar world. Macro economic stabilization and structural adjustment policies (SAP), advocated by multi-lateral agencies like the World Bank (WB) and the International Monetary Fund (IMF), are the components of globalization. These components are either accepted by the countries globalized by membership in the global bodies like the WB, the IMF, the GATT (the WTO since 1995) or are imposed on them. For example, the Government of India declared its New Economic Policy (NEP) in 1991 as a condition of this SAP (Bhalla 1995). The NEP, 1991, aimed at ensuring a 'much freer play of market forces' (GOI, 1991).

The NEP was supposed to have implications on the location of labour vis-à-vis capital. Families are the immediate suppliers of labour while they are the remote suppliers of capital. Capital comes to its controllers (firms) through financial institutions that collect savings (money) from the families. However, the participation of the workers comes through the existence and operations of firms. These firms control both capital and labour, and coordinate between these in the sphere of production. The individual as a labourer sells her labour power where the firm, as the owner or controller of capital, agrees to buy it. This, at the same time, shows the control of capital over labour.

The integration of the economies around the world through the globalization agenda aims at non-discrimination between home and foreign firms. The countries like India generally depend for technologies and investment on foreign firms. 'Non-discrimination' in the globalization agenda means offering 'home treatment' for foreign firms in the host country where the home firm is located. A cordial relationship between foreign firms and home firms on the home soil means also rationalization of firms through a number of means. These means may include technological upgradation, shifting control of capital from the public to the private, downsizing of workers etc. These may again lead to informalization of the labour force and decline of labour power in two ways, one through decline of trade unionism, and the other through decline in real wage rate. Both these ways are inter-linked; the latter follows the reduced bargaining power of labour vis-à-vis capital. The assumptions of the paper are the following:

(i) We consider labour as input in production just as capital (non-labour) is. The expression of this labour-power (a commodity that is offered by a worker for sale and consented to be bought by the controller of capital) is labour hour. This labour hour gets concrete shape in products produced in a firm/farm.

(ii) We consider a worker as an individual who does any job/work independent of the time rule (labour hour) and collects/produces goods for herself (including her family). The worker always exists as a social category, while labour exists as an economic category.

(iii) It needs institutions to convert a social category into an economic category, hence, to convert a worker into a labour/labourer.

(iv) There is at least one individual behind 'work' that is performed on nature, while there has to be at least two individuals for operationalization of 'labour'.

We are going to examine two propositions: (i) The occupational pattern being heavily weighted in favour of land-based activities in the locality, the scope for workers getting converted into 'global labour' is limited. (ii) The conversion of socio-cultural families into economic individuals can convert a local worker into a global labourer.

Job Opportunities and Informalization of Global Labour

Increasing job opportunities, and hence increasing labour mobility, is an integral part of the formation of 'global labour'. The changes in technology, particularly the electronic speed of work, have given birth to a new pattern of work organization from the side of controllers of capital. With respect to technologies moving in an ascending order, thereby saving production (labour) time, there has come a task for both the actual and the potential workers to acquire multi-skills in addition to upgradation in the skill that the worker acquired while joining the current job (ILO, 1997-98). The generation of more advanced technology globally with information transmitted locally has reduced the importance of workers' proximity to the final market for the product.

People were mobile, independent of the globalization agenda, in the pre-Second World War period. This was not only because of trade but also curiosity to know the rest of the world. The discoveries since the 15th century, in particular, of countries through the sea route, bear testimony to this globalization. The rules regarding passport and visa are of recent origin and, in fact, restrict the free movement of people. There is also another type of movement of people, that is, the 'drawing' of people as slaves and indentured labourers from the countries conquered and colonized. The non-occurrence of 'coming back' of the people who moved out willingly and the people who were 'drawn out' came to be used in the sphere of production and related activities in the countries where they 'moved in' or were 'drawn in'. This, at a later stage, came to be recorded as components of labour force of foreign origin. In any case, the use of foreign-born labour force is an indication of global labour, among many other indicators (Table 1).

Table 1

Foreign-born Labour Force in OECD Countries (As percentage of total labour force, Selected Years)

Foreign-born Labour Force in	*1990*	*1997*
US	9.4	10.8*
UK	3.3	3.6
France	6.2	6.1
Germany	7.1	9.1
Japan	0.2	1.0
Italy	-	1.7
Canada	18.5	18.5*
Austria	7.4	9.9
Belgium	-	7.9
Denmark	-	3.1
Ireland	2.6	3.4
Luxembourg	45.2	55.1
Netherlands	3.1	2.9
Norway	2.3	2.8
Portugal	1.0	1.8
Spain	0.6	1.1
Sweden	5.4	5.2
Switzerland	18.9	17.5
Australia	-	24.5

*Data relate to 1996

Source: ILO, 2001, World Employment Report, p. 19.

Implications of Table 1

First, because of use of slaves in the remote past and their ultimate settlement in countries like the US, the percentage of foreign-born labour remains high even now.

Second, the high share of foreign-born labour in total labour employment may show more of intra-OECD adjustment in labour force that limits ethnic composition of workers and hence, invites lesser ethnic conflicts in the OECD countries.

Third, for countries like Canada, this may be because of initial necessity to cover by production huge territorial areas, particularly for agricultural purposes, and hence, the high percentage of foreign-born labour in Canada may reflect the initial open-door policy for entry of labour from abroad.

Fourth, the percentage as a whole for all the countries in OECD may fail to show a high percentage of labour settled in these counties that continue to move out from the Third World countries. The TWCs have around three-fourth of the world population. If, as a rough approximation, one-third of this population is in the working age, then one-fourth of the world population will be available in the TWCs as population in the working age. The OECD countries, as a whole, have population less than one-fourth of world population, implying that the OECD countries may provide the job space for, at most, one-twelfth of the world population. It is an absurd idea that the OECD countries will provide space for even this one-twelfth of world population, that is, one-third of settled population in the working age in the TWCs.

The OECD countries, thus, can not continue to be a destination for the population in the working age in the TWCs. This is not to imply that there should not be any 'globally competent' person seeking absorption in any of the OECD countries, or creating scope for movement across OECD countries.

Implications of Table 2

Prime facie, the data for all the countries based on regional average show similar rates of labour force participation. India conforms to this pattern. The data show nothing more than a size of population in the specified age bracket that deems to be economically active. What the data fail to capture is the very nature of employment. In the less developed regions comprising countries in Asia (excluding Japan), Africa and Latin America, most of the people remain dependent on land (agriculture). The social structure in most of these countries being accommodative and the economic structure being pre-capitalistic, the people in the working age remain less mobile. Underemployment or low-productivity based employment is the corollary.

Table 2

Labour Force Participation Rates at Age 15-64, 1980-2000 (Selected Years)

Region/Country	*1980*	*1995*	*2000*
World	72.6	73.0	73.3
More developed regions	71.4	72.7	73.1
Less developed regions	73.1	73.4	73.4
Least developed regions	78.7	77.2	76.8
India	68.9	66.4	66.6

Source : ILO, 2000, World Labour Report, pp. 267-268.

Ground Reality

Most of the population of both working and non-working age (children and aged) in the Third World countries depends on agriculture for mere survival. The questions related to the pattern of labour employment like part-time, casual etc. are meaningless in most of these cases. In a large country like India by size of total population, and hence population in the working age, this means absence of any choice for the individuals in families other than being dependent on land. All the Census data since 1961 on percentage distribution of the workforce in rural India have shown hardly any change for both male and female. For male workers the percentage varies between 76.0 and 81.0 per cent and for female workers it varies between 84.0 and 88.0 per cent. The National Sample Survey (NSS), which has followed comparable definitions on employment and unemployment, shows a similar trend (NIRD, 1999, p. 55-56). The economic life of most of the population is really embedded in its socio-cultural life. For most of the population it is ritual, or the tradition, that determines whether the economic practices can be at all pursued. These rituals and tradition-based practices are really reflections of caste and gender dependent exclusive practices. Production in any locality, generally a village or cluster of villages, is often not based on monetary exchange. Either it is for self-consumption or for sharing within the locality, whether or not barter-based. In absence of 'production for money-based exchange' the products that come out from land-cum-unskilled labour remain generally unprocessed or less processed. The consequences are obvious. In absence of technological change, or in a state of ignorance about technological change elsewhere, or inability or unwillingness to apply the advanced state of technology, the production structure remains primitive and localized. It also leads to low land-cum-labour productivity. There is fear that technological change when applied might lead to displacement of a section of the initial 'wage workers'. The second one also may imply surrender (leasing-out) of small plots of land to the big landholders, because advanced technology happens to be too costly for the very small farmer, by size of land holding and the capacity to input-use, to adopt.

Underemployment

The calculation, theoretically, on the size of underemployment or disguised employment, does not lead us too far. Whether or not dependent directly on land, it is generally accommodative family labour where the distinction between the buyer and the seller of labour power is blurred. Even if, thus, the number of days in any particular year (less than 180 working days) is taken as the basis of identifying the underemployed worker, in practice it becomes rarely possible. First, it is not very clear what section of the workers engaged at present will be declared surplus and, then, what consequence they will face. Second, who is going to declare them surplus and then work as a catalyst to reemploy them? Third, if it is productivity (marginal, which is not applied on the field) calculated for existing workers, there may come a 'technology solution' whereby the existing capitalist farmers will try to rationalize their firms by 'hire and fire'. The question remains for most of the non-capitalist firms in economies like India where workers are socially-culturally accommodated in the economic space also.

Identification of the Worker

There is no single work for many of the workers. This is not to be read as diversification of jobs that a worker chooses to perform. There is, in fact, no choice for the worker other than trying to minimize the vulnerability by maximizing the number of days she gets the opportunity to work. This work opportunity is also not always clear unless she moves in a state of uncertainty to offer her skill anywhere. While this may lead to the problem of identification of the worker, it also complicates the calculations discussed so far. While land productivity can be measured by physical volume of output, worker productivity may be made fuzzy by price manipulations. In case of multiple jobs, often by distress as opposed to diversification, income-criteria is thought of to identify the worker. Thus, if individual X is self-employed in agricultural work for eight months a year and earns Rs. 20,000 in total, while she works in a mill for four months as casual worker and earns Rs.20,001, she will be called a casual (wage) worker (freeter). If X works for six months a year in agriculture and earns Rs. 15,000 while in a mill she works six months to earn Rs. 30,000 she will, for sure, be called a casual (wage) worker. In the former case, we need to take care of the time spent in agricultural activities and in both the cases we need to take care of the attachment of the individual to land. The point is that whatever temporary job the individual selects, she is land-based for not only earning but also for stable living. Hence, it will be more rational to identify the worker as an agricultural worker, whether she is self-employed in agriculture or employed by others. In case of self-employment, this argument will invite fewer debates.

Economic dynamics take a particular shape when the prevailing mode of production is pre-capitalistic (that is, a hierarchic arrangement of people in the social ladder, people interacting by visible personal relations) and a different shape when it is capitalistic (that is, impersonal social relations indicated by the invisible market). In the former, revealed physical force works, rationalized by 'tradition', 'precedence', 'convention' etc. while in the latter, coercion is hidden under the guise of market forces (for example, via exclusion of people not possessing any marketable property or exit of people by the forces of the market). In the former, people are included by caste-custom-prejudice etc. while in the latter people are included on the basis of money (Majumder, 1997). For most of the workers traditionally depending on land, as in the non-capitalist agricultural regions in India, the economic division of labour lives essentially in the womb of the caste division of labour. In this frame the workers feel comfortable to move out from land (agriculture) to land (agriculture). This may be one reason why there often occurs movement of workers from rural Bihar to rural Punjab, and movement of workers from rural Orissa to rural Gujarat. The familiarity of the new environment (including job environment), historically-culturally, and not necessarily by wage negotiations, helps this movement.

Workers and Work Opportunities in a 'Local-Regional' Economy

In localized economies of most of the underdeveloped countries, family bondage works more than the mobility of the individual in the working age. The family as a whole provides income security. It is a collective/accommodative economy where family priorities come ahead of the individual's self-priorities. The family is the economic unit, not the individual. The revealed choices of an individual are really the reflection of simultaneous decisions of all members in the family that attempt to optimize family welfare, with the gains and losses of all the members of the family entering into the decision. Decisions on migration are no exception.

Often people settled in an underdeveloped region move in a state of limited knowledge about job opportunities. This limited knowledge is derived from past practices of the same individual or the practices of her past generations. The small underdeveloped locality offers limited social safety and insignificant economic safety. The individual, depending on the socio-cultural characteristics of both the localities 'moving out' and 'moving in', moves with and without families. The 'twin localities' show scope for work for the 'moved out' and the moved in' individual. This is not the same as wage-differential determined labour mobility. Generally people settled in villages in underdeveloped regions prefer to stay inside the villages by attachment to land, other animals, relatives, and local environment in its totality. The cultural factors like language, rituals also, reinforce this tendency to remain attached to the locality. In fact, in such localities, land-based activities remain symbols of broader life, and not simply an economic occupation.

While the society-cum-culture works as bondage for the individual, non-development of the local economy drives the individual out. A mismatch between economic compulsions and socio-cultural taboos that often prevail in underdeveloped localities may drive the individuals out. The individual moved out thus may become an economic individual when she 'moves in' to an economic job elsewhere. Let us present a few examples.

Example 1: It is not necessarily true that the locality of an income-cum-asset poor individual is the village for economic purposes. The individual moves to regions for economic survival of her family not only outside the village where she is settled by birth but even beyond her national orbit. During pre-monsoon and monsoon months (June-Sept), the income-cum-asset poor individuals move out of Bangladesh and enter West Bengal, particularly in and around Kolkata, in search of jobs. These people mend umbrellas in which they have skill by heredity practices. They know the local language where they 'move in' and accommodated. They go back to Bangladesh after they have earned income in cash.

Example 2: People are brought from the Nwada region of the state of Bihar generally in families to work as workers in the brick plants located at a distance from Kolkata in West Bengal. These income-cum-asset poor people work for around six months (Oct-March) a year, live in temporary sheds inside the brick plant; they earn income in cash and go back at the end of the production period. One 'Munshiji' (labour contractor) is generally used to bring these workers for which the contractor is paid cash in advance by the owner of the plant. A part of this initial payment is distributed among the heads of the 'drawn out' families even before the workers are absorbed in the brick plants. This is supposed to ensure security for the rest of the members of the families 'drawn out' from the villages in Bihar. This movement of workers could be from anywhere to anywhere. Often it is directionless.

Example 3: The high-caste landless individual may face socio-cultural barriers when he likes to be hired by others to do a manual (menial) job inside the same or adjoining village in East Uttar Pradesh. The individual moves out to Kolkata. He works as a taxi driver earning well and gets settled there. This is culture-led forced migration. The type of job that this individual does in Kolkata because of the anonymous character of a metropolitan city could not be possible in the villages in an underdeveloped region and even in the small towns where the high caste individual has root by birth.

Example 4: The individual who got settled in Jadavpur area, adjacent to Kolkata, long back since his early years selling cheap snacks on the road-side mobile stall had to come back to the village adjacent to the city of Allahabad in Uttar Pradesh. The individual has come back to his native village. The individual continues to do the same job, that is, selling cheap snacks prepared on a mobile stall with a 'chullah' fixed inside on the road-side of the city of Allahabad. The individual, along with his family, stays in the village at a distance of around 10 k.m. from the city, 'moves in' the city every day in the morning and 'moves out' in the afternoon. He had to come back from Kolkata that offered him higher earnings per day, because the Government of West Bengal took the decision to reconstruct roads-cum-pavements and hence the individual could not take any chance to be again rehabilitated there. Nor could he wait to be rehabilitated.

In all the cases, it is the survival instinct of the individuals and families that matters in taking decisions regarding economic activities, often under compulsions. The examples that we have cited do not show any uniform pattern in terms of income/wage received and other practices by utilization of time per day. However, all of them show a situation of initial income-cum-asset poverty, absence of conversion of the locality considered as a socio-cultural unit into an open economic unit, and hence, for some individuals and families the urgency to 'move out'. In general, the written formal contracts governing the economic exchanges between buyers and sellers, and between employers and employees, are absent in such movements because of pre-capitalistic institutional arrangements.

Labour Mobility vis-à-vis Workers' Search for Jobs

Capital is mobile because of decisions by the controllers of capital. The financial institutions as custodians of capital follow the users of capital. The knowledge of workers can move at an electronic speed, but not the worker herself. The way the workers get affected by the utilization of capital and other factors are obviously not the same as the way the capital and other inanimate factors are affected. The way labour, capital, and other factors are affected, are linked with factors like market size, technology, access to market etc. Many of these determining factors are also linked with 'workers' decisions at multi levels and layers.

The mobility discussed in literature often rules out dual existence of man. The individual as an economic agent is assumed to be not a casual (part-time) worker, nor does she share jobs in exchange of income of any type seasonally/occasionally. She is assumed not to be in distress to sell anything that she may be collecting from common resources. She is assumed to have saleable labour (labour-power as a commodity) for which she readily finds a buyer. This shows a very limited frame of analyzing workers' (often potentially existing) economic existence and mobility.

Immobility and Restricted Mobility of Workers

The industrially less developed countries, in general, are characterized by immobility of workers. This is not because of the unwillingness of the workers to be mobile but because they are not informed about 'better' job opportunities elsewhere. Even when jobs of any type are available and known to the worker, she may not be in a position to be present everywhere because of the initial cost involved, like travel cost and costs for many other necessities.

The worker calculates a trade off between benefits that the new job will provide her and the costs that she will have to incur. These costs are not visibly always monetary. The non-wage factors include the accommodation of the worker's family, the education of the children in a new region with all new linguistic-cultural implications, the service facilities in the new region, the existing occupation of the spouse, the dependents in the family etc.

Often the hiring of workers in a less industrialized economy is hiring of all the members in the family. This may be seen in construction works supervised by a contractor, generally in an urban area. This may also be seen in brick-kilns located generally in rural areas adjacent to a final (urban) market where workers are brought from distant rural areas. The urban owners or plant managers of the brick kilns take the help of a contractor ('Munshiji'), generally with knowledge of rural areas, to get the family labour hired. Both these types of workers are employed seasonally. While in the former case it is for a temporary period (depending on the cost-benefit calculations of the labour contractor), in case of the latter it is season-specific (Oct-March). These family workers are not self-employed, but employed by others and in the informal sector. Temporary/seasonal employment for a period does not guarantee job opportunities for periods to come. If the job to come in the next period is not known, any future movement of these workers remains uncertain and footloose. There may remain a big geographic distance between the spaces where these workers expect to get jobs. These workers, being economically vulnerable, can not bear the cost of moving in a state of uncertainty. Hence, they are taken forward by the labour contractors for any future job settlements. These workers, thus, are not really mobile, but show the characteristics of indentured labourers.

On the assumption that the initial absorption of workers in a particular plant was rational, it will be rational for a firm to discourage the exit of skilled workers. There is, thus, internal obstruction for a worker's mobility. This obstruction is not always visible. The same firm, however, encourages the entry of workers who have proved themselves skilled in other plants, thereby inviting mobility. The prevailing technology does not throw workers out, but the improving technology shows the path of eviction of a section of workers. This is to be contrasted with mobility of workers. Training of workers by job rotation inside a plant, or at an inter-firm level, shows shift of workers, and not necessarily mobility by promotion. The project-specific displacement is independent of the choice of the people in the working age, along with their families. The eviction of settled people from the land is another example of displacement. These workers may seek jobs anywhere in the national economy, or, even outside the national boundary. The people in the working age may shift to the neighbouring country, independent of the choice of the affected people, because of war, partition etc. and seek jobs in the new settled region.

Engagement in a number of jobs does not always show stability by reduced vulnerability in 'one job', but may show vulnerability of the worker herself when the single initial job is not dependable. In a conventional sense, this dependability is subject to the existing market conditions and, hence, the return that the job offers throughout the year and over the years. In reality, the initial job that the individual is thrown into becomes fait accompli where she gets attached since her childhood. It may be land-related jobs; it may be any job in the unorganized sector. Natural calamities in the former by flood, drought and absence of any protection of workers through labour laws etc. in the latter, keep the workers vulnerable.

The workers' resistance to new entry in the organized sector may obstruct worker's mobility. This obstruction is really for those who like to move within the organized sector. Often inter-firm mobility of workers may be obstructed by political influence. Mobility of workers may also be constrained by non-innovative or stereotype jobs, where internal workers 'do the job'. Often the entry of individuals into the job market is 'time-tied', making workers' mobility non-operational for a stipulated period. Some types of entry may be delinked from any guarantee of jobs, for example, Apprenticeship Schemes. Any mobility from the informal to the formal sector is an uphill task. Often an attempt toward this may show slumization and deruralization (Breman, 2003).

Concluding Comments

The task is to convert social categories into economic categories. In the context of labour, it means conversion of caste division of labour into economic division of labour. This reveals both the inner weaknesses in a system and the need to reorient the system. A positive step towards exposing the problem of unemployment and underemployment would be to plan for training, job-rotation, and placement of the workers on jobs that are based on and consistent with the knowledge base of these workers. Development of agriculture-related activities on an industrial basis, development of rural infrastructure, and development of local resource-based rural industries are the major routes by which these populations can be productively settled. The state has to be the catalyst for these.

References

Bhalla, G. S. (1995), "Globalization and Agricultural Policy in India", *Indian Journal of Economics*, Vol. L, NO. 1, Jan-March.

Breman, Jan, (2003), "Globalization poverty and Exclusion", G. B. Pant Memorial Lecture delivered in G. B. Pant Social Science Institute, Allahabad, Oct. 20-22.

GOI, (1991), "Ministry of External Affairs", India's New Economic Policies, New Delhi.

ILO, (1997-98), "World Labour Report", Geneva.

ILO, (2000), "World Labour Report", Geneva.

ILO, (2001), "World Employment Report", Geneva.

Majumder Bhaskar, (1997), "Accommodating New Economic Policy in India's Social Dynamics: A Critical Review", *Productivity*, Vol. 37, No. 4, Jan-March.

National Institute of Rural Development (NIRD) (1999), "India Rural Development Report", Hyderabad.

5

Labour in a Globalised World and Workers in a Localised Economy: Employment and Mobility

The post-Second World War is globalised in a bipolar world while the post-Cold War world is globalised in a unipolar world. Macro-economic stabilization and structural adjustment policies (SAP) advocated by multilateral agencies like the World Bank (WB) and the International Monetary Fund (IMF) show the components of globalization. These components are either accepted by the countries that are globalised by membership in the global bodies like WB, the IMF, the GATT (now the WTO since 1995) or are imposed on them. For example, the Government of India declared its New Economic Policy (NEP) in 1991 as a part (condition) of this SAP (Bhalla, 1995, p. 7). The purpose of the GOI, while announcing the NEP in 1991, was 'to unshackle the industrial economy from the cobwebs of unnecessary bureaucratic control' (GOI, 1991, p. 6). It also aimed at ensuring 'much freer play of market forces' (ibid, p. 5).

The NEP was supposed to have implications on workers' participation in a new paradigm. This participation comes through the existence and operations of firms. Globalization generally depends for technologies and investment on foreign firms. Non-discrimination means offering 'home treatment' to foreign firms in the host country where the home firm is located. A cordial relationship between foreign firms and home firms on home soil also implies the rationalization of firms through a number of means. These means may include technological upgradation, downsizing workers, etc. These may again lead to the informalisation of the labour force and decline of labour power in two ways: one through the decline of trade unionism, and the other through a decline in the real wage rate.

In this paper, we are not considering these entire complex and chain consequences of globalization of labour/workers. We consider labour as an input in production just as capital (non-labour) is. The expression of this labour-power (a commodity that is offered by a worker for sale and consented to be bought by another worker) is labour hour. This labour hour acquire a concrete shape in the products produced in a firm/farm. This again shows labour productivity per unit of time. We consider the worker as an individual who does any job/work independent of the time rule (labour hour) and collects/produces goods for herself (including her family). The worker always exists as a social category, while labour exists as an economic category. There is need for institutions to convert a social category into an economic category, and hence to convert a worker into a labour/labourer. The analysis that follows relies on labour-related information from secondary sources and work-related information from primary sources. There is at least one individual behind 'work' along with nature, while at least two individuals are required for the operationalisation of 'labour'. We concentrate on the actual work practices of population in the working age in the Third World countries, with reference to India. For this we will rely more on primary data that we collected at the micro-level.

This paper has four sections. In Section I, we analyze changing 'labour conditions and job opportunities in the globalised world. In Section II, we deal with workers and work opportunities in a localized economy. In Section III, we pose the question pertaining to labour mobility vis-à-vis workers' mobility. Finally, in Section IV, we offer concluding comments.

(I) Changing Labour Conditions and Job Opportunities in the Globalised World

Increasing job opportunities, and hence increasing labour mobility, is an integral part of the formation of the 'global man'. The changes in technology, particularly the electronic speed of work, have given birth to a new pattern of work organization from the employers' side. "The changing character of new technologies requires workers who can learn and adapt to these changes quickly and efficiently. Although the skill itself may not be 'higher', the ability to master it quickly and use it productively calls for a high level of confidence and familiarity that favours the higher skilled" (ILO, 1997-98, p. 46). With respect to emerging technologies in an ascending order, thus, it has become necessary for a potential worker to acquire multi-dimensional skills in addition to upgrading the skill that s/he acquired while joining the current job. The use of more advanced technology globally facilitating the transmission of information locally has reduced the importance of workers' proximity to the final market for the product. Even for the provision of more services, proximity has become irrelevant. "For example, software development in Bangalore, India, has skyrocketed in a brief, ten-year period. The engineers are highly skilled, earnings are a fraction of the United States or German salaries, and the 'product' –software - can be delivered anywhere in the world in real time at the push of a button" (ILO, 1997-98, p. 86). The globalised labour market is also manifested in the foreign labour force engaged in the developed capitalist countries (Table 1).

For the very small economy by size of population such as Luxembourg, the foreign labour force absorbed as a percentage of the total labour force, was very high during the 1990s. For a small country by size of population such as Switzerland, this percentage was also high. The pattern may imply many things. Firstly, because of the initial use of slaves and their ultimate settlement in countries like the US, the percentage of foreign-born

Table 1

Foreign-born Labour Force in OECD Countries
(As a Percentage of the Total Labour Force, Selected Year)

Country	*1990*	*1997*
US	9.4	10.8*
UK	3.3	3.6
France	6.2	6.1
Germany	7.1	9.1
Japan	0.2	1.0
Italy	-	1.7
Canada	18.5	18.5*
Austria	7.4	9.9
Belgium	-	7.9
Denmark	-	3.1
Ireland	2.6	3.4
Luxembourg	45.2	55.1
Netherlands	3.1	2.9
Norway	2.3	2.8
Portugal	1.0	1.8
Spain	0.6	1.1
Sweden	5.4	5.2
Switzerland	18.9	17.5
Australia	-	24.6

Note: *Data relate to 1996.
Source: ILO (2001), p. 19.

labour remains high even now. Secondly, this high foreign-born labour percentage may show more of intra-OECD adjustment in the labour force that limits the ethnic composition of workers and hence invites lesser ethnic conflicts. Thirdly, for countries like Canada, this may be because of the initial necessity to cover a huge territorial area by production, particularly for agricultural purposes, and hence the high percentage of foreign-born labour in Canada may reflect the initial open-door policy for the entry of labour from abroad. Fourthly, the percentage as a whole for all the countries in OECD may fail to show a high percentage of labour settled in these countries that continue to move from the Third World countries. The reason for this is that the Third World Countries (TWCs) account for around three-fourths of the world population. If as a rough approximation, one-third of this population is in the working age, then one-fourth of the world working population will be available in the TWCs. The OECD countries as a whole account for less than one-fourth of the world population, implying that the OECD countries may provide the job space for at most one-twelfth of the world population. It will be absurd to suggest that the OECD countries will provide space for even this one-twelfth of the world population, that is, one-third of the settled population in the working age in the TWCs. This is not to imply that there should not be any 'globally competent' person seeking absorption in any of the OECD countries, or creating scope for movement across OECD countries. For example, "in Canada during the 1990s, immigrants accounted for about a third of the increase in employment among computer engineers, systems analysts and computer programmers. Around a quarter of the heads of Silicon Valley companies were born outside the United States. New regulations in Germany, effective from August 2000, allow the entry of 20,000 computing specialists over a period of three years, and the United Kingdom has proposed similar measures to alleviate ICT and other skill shortages. India, Eastern Europe and North Africa are likely to be among the main sources of supply" (ILO, 2001, pp. 18-19).

"Three transformations – the waves of white-collar downsizing in the 1980s and 1990s, the rise in the proportion of value added by skilled workers and the use of ICT - have combined to create a new kind of worker—demanding, mobile and self-reliant. These workers develop a network of contracting arrangements and move quickly between jobs. For them, job choice is driven by a desire to achieve 'labour market' rather than 'employment' security through robust employability skills and good access to ongoing opportunities, rather than single-job security. Some jump from one employer to another—while maintaining networks that transcend any single job or company—others become self-employed freelancers" (ILO, 2001, pp. 112-113).

In the recent past, "all industrialized countries have seen the secular growth of 'non-standard work arrangements', such as temporary jobs, part-time jobs and self-employment. For example, Japan shows a rise in the cases of 'Freeter, that is, the section of people in the working age who choose their work as part-time casual work. This is not in reality a choice, because it was found that 60 percent of these 'freeters' were unable to find more secure employment. In fact, the ILO study on a large sub-set of OECD countries finds that stability of employment continues to be the dominant pattern" (ILO, 2001, p. 114).

The world economies by development categories show similar employment patterns for the last two decades (Table 2).

Table 2

Labour Force Participation Rates at Age 15-64, 1980-2000 (Selected Years)

Region/Country	*1980*	*1995*	*2000*
World	72.6	73.0	73.3
More developed regions	71.4	72.7	73.1
Less developed regions	73.1	73.2	73.4
Least developed regions	78.7	77.2	76.8
India	68.9	66.4	66.6

Note: Labour force participation rates are calculated as a percentage of those in the labour force at age 15-64 to the total population at age 15-64. The population in this age bracket is considered as an economically active population.

Source : ILO (2000), pp. 267-268.

Prima facie, the data for all the countries based on regional average show similar rates of labour force participation. India conforms to this pattern. The data show nothing more than a size of population in the specified age brackets that deem to be economically active. What the data fail to capture is the very nature of employment in the less developed regions comprising countries in Asia (excluding Japan), Africa and Latin America wherein the people remain dependent on land (agriculture). With the social structure in most of these countries being accommodative and the economic structure being pre-capitalistic, the people in the working age remain less mobile. Under-employment or low-productivity based employment is the corollary. Not only are the people in the working age (15-64) economically active in these countries, but the children in the age bracket 5-15, are also economically active. The children are active in workplaces both in separation from their parents and in association with their parents/ other relatives. The work areas are land-based and other local areas, resource-based. As long as the people survive, particularly in the rural areas characterized by agriculture and allied activities, the people remain economically active. No job security and no knowledge implementation of labour laws are relevant in this type of work place. The workers as such in the less developed manual labour-based, often family labour-based, enterprises/regions have nowhere to go except being self-dragged on the land. Land cannot resist the person from being used/employed. The individual in the working age apparently employed on land thus becomes a worker. The person remains a worker because s/he fails to be a seller of labour through the market. In the absence of any alternative job opportunities, or what in conventional literature is called opportunity cost, it does not make much sense to show that the participation rate of the less developed regions, including India, is the same as that of the developed regions.

Any question related to labour employment globally carries operational meaning when the facts revealed in the developed capitalist countries (OECD) are juxtaposed vis-à-vis the often concealed facts (non-recorded/non-disseminated) in the TWCs.

Most of the population in both working and non-working age (children and aged) in the Third World countries depends on agriculture for mere survival. The questions related to the pattern of labour employment like part-time, casual, etc. are meaningless in most of these cases. In a large country like India, by size of total population, and hence population in the working age, this means the absence of any choice for individuals in families other than being dependent on land. The entire Census data since 1961 on the percentage distribution of the workforce in rural India have shown hardly any change for both male and female workers. For male workers, the percentage varies between 76 and 81 per cent and for female workers, it varies between 84 and 88 per cent. The National Sample Survey (NSS), which has followed comparable definitions on employment and unemployment, shows a similar trend (NIRD, 1999, pp. 55-56). The consequences are obvious. Without technological change, it means reducing land-cum-labour productivity, while with technological change, it means the displacement of a section of the initial 'wage workers'. The second possibility may also imply the surrender (leasing-out) of small plots of land to the big landholders, because technology happens to be too costly for the very small farmer to adopt, both by the size of land and the capacity of input-use.

The calculation, theoretically, on the size of under-employment or disguised employment does not lead us too far. Firstly, it is not very clear what section of the workers engaged at present will be declared surplus and then what consequences they will face. Secondly, who is going to declare them surplus and then work as a catalyst to re-employ them? Thirdly, if it is productivity (marginal, which is not applied on the field) calculated for existing workers, the result could be a 'technology solution' whereby the existing capitalist farmers will try to rationalize their farms by 'hire and fire'. The question remains for most of the non-capitalist farms in economies like India where workers are more than economic individuals and hence where they are also socially-culturally accommodated in the economic space.

The problems become more complicated when it is not a single work for many of the workers. While this may lead to the problem of identification of the worker, it also complicates the calculations that we have discussed so far. While land productivity can be measured by the physical volume of output, worker productivity may be made fuzzy by price manipulations. In fact, the entire income (productivity) of workers in the service sector is a reflection of this price manipulation. In case of multiple jobs, often by selection by distress as opposed to diversification, the income criteria are used to identify the worker. Thus, if individual X is self-employed in agricultural work for eight months a year and earns a total of Rs. 20,000, while he works in a mill for four months as a casual worker and earns Rs. 20,001, she will be called a casual (wage) worker ('freeter'). If X works for six months a year in agriculture and earns Rs. 15, 000, while in a mill s/he works six months to earn Rs. 30,000, s/he will certainly be called a casual (wage) worker. In the former case, we need to take care of the time spent in agricultural activities and in both the cases we need to take care of the attachment of the individual to land. The point is that whatever temporary job the individual selects, s/he is land-based for not only earning but also for stable living. Hence, it will be more rational to identify the worker as an agricultural worker, irrespective of whether s/he is self-employed in agriculture or employed by others. In case of self-employment, this argument will invite fewer debates, while in case of hired employment, it will invite debate. Let us then clarify our position for the second case.

The motion of men and materials conditions economic dynamics. This dynamics takes a particular shape when the prevailing mode of production is pre-capitalistic (that is, a hierarchical arrangement of people in the social ladder, people interacting by visible personal relations) and a different shape when it is capitalistic (that is, impersonal social relations indicated by the invisible market). In the former, revealed physical force works, rationalized by 'tradition', 'precedence', 'convention', etc., while in the latter, coercion is hidden under the guise of market forces (for example, via the exclusion of people not possessing any marketable property or the exit of people by the forces of market). In the former, people are included by caste-custom-prejudice, etc., while in the latter, people are included on the basis of money (Majumder, 1997, p. 641). For most of the workers traditionally depending on land, as in the non-capitalist agricultural regions in India, the economic division of labour lives essentially in the womb of the caste division of labour. In this frame, the workers feel comfortable in moving from land (agriculture) to land (agriculture). This may be one reason why the movement of workers often occurs from rural Bihar to rural Punjab, and from rural Orissa to rural Gujarat. The familiarity of the new environment (including job environment) historically-culturally, and not necessarily by wage negotiations, helps this movement.

(II) Workers and Work Opportunities in a Localized Economy

In the localized economies of most of the under-developed countries, family bondage works often more than the mobility of the individual in the working age. The family as a whole provides income security. It is a collective/accommodative economy where family priorities come ahead of individual's self-priorities. The family is the economic unit, not the individual. The revealed choices of an individual are really the reflection of simultaneous decisions of all members in the family that attempt to optimize family welfare, with the gains and losses of all the members of the family entering into the decision. Decisions on migration are no exception (Fearn, 1981, p. 236). In countries in Asia and Africa, the family as a unit remains very important for employment and migration (ILO, 2000, p. 24). The members in the family take care of food security of all the members, care of the children and protection of the disabled and elderly. In this situation, the per capita availability of food comes down along with the per capita production in these localized economies. Many of these local economies may not also show a uniform pattern of work opportunities and conditions of workers. A region like Kerala in India shows more mobility of workers relative to many other regions within the same national economy. A region like Bihar shows more shifts of workers, often poverty-driven, to adjoining regions like West Bengal and also to remote regions like Punjab, relative to workers in Uttar Pradesh. Both the compulsions and propensity to go beyond the small boundary of potentially available jobs make a section of workers more prone to moving relative to others. It is thus necessary to obtain ideas about works, workers, and work opportunities based on the study of a particular region.

Table 3

Occupational Structure of Workers in Allahabad and UP, 1991

Occupation	*Allahabad*	*UP*
Main workers, of which	30.42	29.73
(a) Cultivators	41.31	53.27
(b) Agricultural labourers	22.07	18.94
(c) Livestock and allied activities	0.62	0.71
(d) Mining and quarrying	0.40	0.08
(e) Household industry@	4.32	2.41
(f) Non-Household industry@@	5.83	5.34
(g) Construction	1.13	1.23
(h) Trade and commerce	7.92	6.17
(i) Transport and communication	2.54	1.86
(j) Other services	13.85	9.98
Marginal workers	1.78	2.47
Non-workers	67.79	67.80
Total	100.0	100.0

Note : @ Manufacturing, processing, servicing and repairs in household industry.

@@ Manufacturing, processing, servicing and repairs in industry other than the household industry.

Source : District Statistical Handbook of Allahabad, 1998 and Census of India, 1991, pp. 53-59 (State level data, pp. 605-611; District level data).

While for understanding global labour mobility, the selection of a national economy is the unit, for understanding workers' entry into occupations and mobility in the context of a national economy like India, the selection of a smaller region is a necessity. We select a particular district for this study, viz. the district of Allahabad in Uttar Pradesh, India. This district is one of the developed districts in Uttar Pradesh (UP), located in the eastern part of UP, which is known as an underdeveloped region within UP. The regional distribution of population in the district is 75:25 in terms of the rural: urban division. Let us first see the overall occupational structure of the District along with the state, UP (Table 3).

Thus, around 30 per cent of the total population in the working age constitutes the main workers in the district, which is the same as that of the state. The non-workers constitute around 68 per cent, which is also the same as that of the state. The marginal workers form the rest. In the main workers category, the cultivators constitute the maximum number, followed by agricultural labourers. The questions where changing technology and mobility could be meaningful are non-household industry and services. For an economy like India, more so for its settled population in an underdeveloped region, services show internal limited mobility and external (across countries) general immobility. With the occupational pattern being heavily weighted in favour of land-based activities in the district, the scope for workers getting converted into 'global labour' becomes a rare possibility. To test the hypothesis, we took a sample based on multi-stage purposive sampling.

District Allahabad has 20 development blocks of which we selected four purposively in a geographically dispersed manner. These blocks cover industrially developed, hilly developed and underdeveloped areas of the district. The district has 2,715 inhabited revenue villages and 11 towns. All villages are stratified into three groups by size of population, (i) between 500 and 999, (ii) between 1,000 and 1,999, and (iii) between 2000 and 4,999. We selected a total of 24 villages, six from each block. Of these selected villages, a total of 12, that is, half is selected from category (ii). Thus, we selected more of median villages. We also selected two towns, one of them an industrial area, and the other, a border town that may show trade and associated movement of people. From each town, we selected two wards, that is, we selected a total of four wards. In the second stage, we selected 50 households from each village as well as 50 households from each ward of a town by income category using the random sampling method. We took care of the income category by ration card holding, that is below poverty line (BPL) and above poverty line (APL). Thus, we selected a total of 1400 households. We know the limitations of such selection by card holding (Majumder, 2001).

We used structured schedules for the households, the respondents being members of the population in the working age. We found very limited movement of these people even outside the boundary of the district for any economic purposes. We found no household in the selected sample that was willing to leave the villages permanently. There occurred some seasonal movement of some semi-skilled individuals to one or two metropolitan cities within India. We did not find global mobility of the population in the working age. So, we tried to capture mobility within the locality and across economic activities (Table 4).

The selected blocks in the district are Shankargarh, Karchhana, Saidabad, and Kurihar. The selected towns are Phulpur and Bharatganj. For all households, the population engaged as cultivators, agricultural labourers, and non-agricultural labourers covers 71.60 per cent of all occupations. There are, however, inter-block and inter-town, and between blocks and towns, variations in the percentage of households engaged in agricultural (as cultivators and labourers) and non-agricultural activities (like non-agricultural labour, government service, etc.). The occupational structure of sample households (1400) shows 8.6 per cent involved in more than one occupation. The households engaged as cultivators constitute 65.4 per cent of the total employment of households in a single sector (agriculture). The households identified as

Table 4

Occupation-wise Distribution of Households in Allahabad by Regions and Towns

Block/town	*Occupation*											
	1	*2*	*3*	*4*	*5*	*6*	*7*	*8*	*9*	*10*	*11*	*Total*
Shankargarh	54 (18.0)	3 (1.0)	191 (63.7)	6 (2.0)	5 (1.7)	11 (3.7)	4 (1.3)	4 (1.3)	19 (6.5)	---	3 (1.0)	300 (100.0)
Karchhana	64 (21.3)	78 (26.0)	72 (24.0)	14 (4.8)	10 (3.3)	19 (6.3)	12 (4.0)	5 (1.7)	22 (7.3)	4 (1.3)	---	300 (100.0)
Saidabad	86 (28.7)	45 (15.0)	68 (22.7)	13 (4.3)	10 (3.3)	11 (3.7)	41 (13.7)	4 (1.3)	17 (5.7)	1 (0.3)	4 (1.3)	300 (100.0)
Kaurihar	46 (15.3)	55 (18.3)	156 (52.0)	2 (0.7)	3 (1.0)	8 (2.7)	5 (1.7)	6 (2.0)	16 (5.3)	1 (0.3)	2 (0.7)	300 (100.0)
Phulpur	3 (3.0)	5 (5.0)	35 (35.0)	4 (4.0)	4 (4.0)	13 (13.0)	23 (23.0)	4 (4.0)	9 (9.0)	---	---	100 (100.0)
Bharatganj	2 (2.0)	3 (3.0)	37 (37.0)	6 (6.0)	3 (3.0)	32 (32.0)	1 (1.0)	1 (1.0)	15 (15.0)	---	---	100 (100.0)
Total	255 (18.2)	189 (18.5)	559 (39.9)	45 (3.2)	35 (2.5)	94 (6.7)	86 (6.1)	24 (1.7)	98 (7.0)	6 (0.4)	9 (0.6)	1400 (100.0)

Note : 1=Cultivator, 2=Agriculture Labour, 3=Non-agriculture labour, 4=Private service, 5=Govt. service, 6=Small business, 7=Artisans, 8=Housewives, 9=Students, 10=Unemployed, 11=Others [*Pujari* (Priest), *Sapera* (Snake Charmer) and Washerman, etc.

Source: Field Survey, 2001.

individuals engaged as cultivators also work in industry/services/ other sectors. The households engaged as agricultural labourers in a single job constitute 28.9 per cent of the total employment in agriculture. Since the economic activities in the sample households mainly belong to agriculture and allied activities, the extent of unemployment is as low as 0.6 per cent of all households involved in a single sector (Table 5).

In terms of the time spent, agriculture constitutes 61.7 per cent of the total time spent (employment) on all occupations recorded for the sample households, with the second rank being that of non-agricultural work at 17.5 per cent. However, if the occupation is identified by income, then the service sector (private and government) accounts for the most (Table 6).

It shows a mixture of occupations by time spent and income earned for the rural households. Although by time spent, agriculture (cultivators and agricultural labourers) is the dominant activity for the sample households, in terms of income earned, there are sharp differences across activities.

Generally the local economic units show an informal nature of employment. In general, the written, formal contracts governing the economic exchanges between buyers and sellers, and between employers and employees are absent because of pre-capitalistic institutional arrangements. "Informal units comprise small enterprises with hired workers, household 'enterprises' using mostly family labour, and the self-employed. Production processes involve relatively high levels of working capital as against fixed capital, which in turn reflects the relatively low level of technology and skills involved. While the small enterprises could well be involved in continuous production processes, most units engage in batch production methods and are seasonal in nature" (ILO, 1998-99, p. 167). The working inability of the workers in plants in the technologically changing circumstances aggravates the situation, if they are absorbed in the formal sector. In India, for example, a large proportion of the labour force is illiterate. "A major part of

Table 5

Occupational Structure of Households

Occupation	*Agriculture*	*Industry*	*Services*	*Other Sector*	*Total*
Cultivators	253 (65.4)	5 (13.5)	20 (21.5)	18 (2.0)	296 (21.1)
Agricultural labour	112 (28.9)	3 (8.1)	3 (3.2)	89 (10.1)	207 (14.8)
Non-agricultural labour	22 (5.7)	18 (48.6)	1 (1.1)	531 (60.1)	572 (40.9)
Private service	1 (0.3)	2 (5.4)	42 (45.2)	6 (0.7)	51 (3.6)
Government Service	9 (2.3)	1 (2.7)	34 (36.6)	1 (0.1)	45 (3.2)
Small business	4 (1.0)	2 (5.4)	4 (4.3)	94 (10.6)	104 (7.4)
Artisans	6 (1.6)	15 (40.5)	3 (3.2)	70 (7.9)	94 (6.7)

(Contd.)

(Contd. Table 5)

Occupation	*Agriculture*	*Industry*	*Services*	*Other Sector*	*Total*
Housewives	9 (2.3)	---	4 (4.3)	13 (1.5)	26 (1.9)
Students	3 (0.8)	---	1 (1.1)	3 (0.3)	7 (0.5)
Unemployed	1 (0.3)	---	2 (2.2)	5 (0.6)	8 (0.6)
Others	17 (4.4)	1 (2.7)	10 (10.6)	82 (9.3)	110 (7.9)
Total	437 (112.9)	47 (127.0)	124 (133.3)	912 (103.3)	1520 (108.6)
Households involved in more than one sector*	50 (12.9)	10 (27.0)	31 (33.3)	29 (3.3)	120 (8.6)
Households involved in a single sector	387 (100.0)	37 (100.0)	93 (100.0)	883 (100.0)	1400 (100.0)

Note : * 1. These households are involved in more than one occupation and they are earning from more than one sector.

2. Figures in brackets are percentages.

Source : Field Survey, 2001.

Table 6

Income and Employment Structure of Households in Terms of Income and Time Spent

Sectoral Occupation	*1*	*2*	*3*	*4*	*5*	*6*	*7*	*Total*
In terms of income								
Cultivators	10 (20.0)	5 (10.0)	3 (6.0)	10 (20.0)	11 (22.0)	4 (8.0)	7 (14.0)	50 (100.0)
Industry	2 (20.0)	---	2 (20.0)	---	---	1 (10.0)	5 (50.0)	10 (100.0)
Services	4 (12.9)	---	---	13 (41.9)	14 (45.2)	---	---	31 (100.0)
Others*	7 (24.1)	5 (17.2)	1 (3.4)	4 (13.8)	3 (10.3)	6 (20.7)	3 (10.3)	29 (100.0)
Total	23 (19.2)	10 (8.3)	6 (5.0)	27 (22.5)	28 (23.3)	11 (9.2)	15 (12.5)	120 (100.0)

(Contd.)

(Contd. Table 6)

Sectoral Occupation	*1*	*2*	*3*	*4*	*5*	*6*	*7*	*Total*
In terms of time spent								
Cultivators	37 (72.0)	2 (4.0)	5 (10.0)	2 (4.0)	1 (2.0)	1 (2.0)	2 (4.0)	50 (100.0)
Industry	4 (40.0)	2 (20.0)	3 (30.0)	---	---	---	1 (10.0)	10 (100.0)
Services	21 (67.7)	1 (3.2)	3 (9.7)	2 (6.4)	1 (3.2)	1 (3.2)	2 (6.4)	31 (100.0)
Others*	12 (41.4)	1 (3.4)	10 (34.5)	1 (3.4)	---	2 (6.9)	3 (10.3)	29 (100.0)
Total	74 (61.7)	6 (5.0)	21 (17.5)	5 (4.2)	2 (1.7)	4 (3.4)	8 (6.7)	120 (100.0)

Note : 1=Cultivator, 2=Agriculture Labour, 3=Non-agriculture labour, 4=Private service, 5=Government service, 6=Small business, 7=Artisans.

*It includes non-agricultural workers, artisans, small shop owners, doctors (unregistered), weavers, washermen, drivers, *madari* (monkey charmers), *purohit* (priests), bandmasters, etc.

Source : Field Survey, 2001.

industry with the exception of a few multinationals and a few large scale employers depends upon informal channels to recruit and train its workforce. While the informal apprenticeship system (*ustaad-shagird*, that is teacher-assistant) has many elements which make it attractive in terms of cheap on-the-job training, the cost in terms of quality and productivity may be high" (ILO, 1998-99, p. 126).

(III) Labour Mobility or Workers' Mobility

The question pertaining to mobility of factors of production in conventional economic analysis treats all factors as similar. Thus, the mobility of labour (measured perhaps by labour hour) is considered along with mobility of capital and treated in a production function in the same way. However, neither as a cause nor as a consequence are they the same.

Capital is mobile because of decisions by workers (these workers may be at the level of authority in a hierarchical frame of production). Even the electronic speed of capital is because of workers who are engaged with the system of electronic communication have the facility of pressing a push button at will. The knowledge of workers can move in an electronic speed, but not the worker herself. The manner in which the workers get affected by the utilization of capital and other factors is obviously not the same as the manner in which capital and other inanimate factors are affected. The way that labour, capital, and other factors are affected is linked with many factors like market size, technology, access to market (trade), etc. Many of these determining factors are also intimately linked with the workers' decisions at multi-levels and layers.

The mobility that is generally discussed in literature stands on inter-industrial mobility. Generally, it rules out the dual existence of man. The individual as an economic agent is assumed to be not a casual (part-time) worker, not does she share jobs in exchange of income of any type seasonally or occasionally. She is assumed not to be in distress to sell anything that she may be collecting from common resources. She is assumed to have saleable labour (labour-power as a commodity) for which she readily finds a buyer. This shows a very limited frame of analyzing workers' (often potentially existing) economic existence and mobility.

The industrially less developed countries are, in general, characterized by the immobility of workers. This is not because of the unwillingness of the workers to be mobile but because they are not informed about 'better' job opportunities elsewhere. We say 'better' job opportunities because mobility is linked with the latter, rather than the worker being compelled to accept any job anywhere in a situation of 'displacement' or 'distress' of the worker and her family. We keep in mind the population in an underdeveloped region/economy in the working age and talk about alternative phrases like 'mobility', 'migration', 'displacement', 'shift', 'eviction', etc. Even when jobs of any type are available, initial cost is involved like travel cost and costs for many other necessities for living. The term 'mobility' implicitly implies vertical movement. It involves higher wages and better working conditions and/or better establishment/status. Both the capability of the individual and job opportunity are relevant for such mobility.

Labour mobility is, thus, conditioned at the starting point by additional job opportunities and subsequently by wage flexibility and wage differential. For the national economy, inter-regional and inter-industry movement may not necessarily show additional job opportunities for additional workers. It may show re-allocation of the same labour (by labour hour and by same number of individuals). Thus, meaningful labour mobility requires income-increasing job opportunities.

A worker joins a job generally independent of her own choice or in conditions of ignorance (Rottenberg, 1968). This worker, initially at a young age, is more of an individual, and less of a member attached to a family, that enables her to go and join a job anywhere. With rising productivity and rising monotony in the initial job, the individual attains the capability to choose another job, that is, she changes the initial job by selecting a new one. By then the individual probably has become a member attached to a family by marital status. The worker calculates a trade-off between benefits that the new job will provide her and the costs that she will have to incur. These costs are not visibly always monetary. Even the worker's knowledge of wage and non-wage terms of employment in other jobs is not sound (Reynolds, 1951, p. 213). It may also be that the worker's mobility is responsive to more non-wage factors and forces than the wage differential, if the latter is really known. These non-wage factors are the accommodation of the worker's family, the education of the children in a new region with all its new linguistic-cultural implications, the existing occupation of the spouse, etc. The mobility of the worker is, thus, sharply different from the supply-side behaviour of labour mobility that corresponds to output, capital intensity (Majumder, 1995, p. 99).

On the assumption that the initial absorption of workers in a particular plant was rational, it will be rational for a firm to discourage the exit of skilled workers. There is, thus, internal obstruction for worker's mobility. This obstruction is not always visible. The same firm, however, encourages the entry of workers who have proved themselves to be skilled in other plants, thereby inviting mobility. No firm employs just one person. It is a production system based on the co-operation of workers with multiple layers of skill. The plant-specific production, thus, shows inter-dependence of the workers employed. The prevailing technology does not throw workers out, but the improving technology shows the path of eviction of a section of workers. This is to be contrasted with the mobility of workers. Training of workers by job rotation inside a plant or at an inter-firm level shows the shift of workers, and not necessarily mobility by promotion. The project-specific displacement, such as construction of roads, dams, etc., may lead to displacement of workers from settled localities affected by these infrastructural initiatives. This displacement is independent of the choice of the people in the working age along with their families. The eviction of settled people from the land they had been cultivating is another example of displacement. These workers may seek jobs anywhere in the national economy, or even outside the national boundary. The people in the working age may shift to a neighbouring country, a country to be settled by determination of state power and independent of the choice of the affected people, because of war, partition, etc. and seek jobs in the new settled region. These people are often called refugees or people who seek asylum. Engagement in a number of jobs does not always show stability by reduced vulnerability in 'one job', but may show the vulnerability of the worker herself when the single initial job is not much dependable. This dependence is subject to the existing market conditions and hence the return that the job offers throughout the year and over a number of years. The Ando-Modigliani type calculation of future income stream from the job itself is unreliable, if the calculation itself is not impossible.

The workers themselves may show inner antagonism in an inter-firm frame so far as labour of one is thought to be substitutable for the other. This may obstruct workers mobility. Often the inter-firm mobility of workers may be obstructed by political influence for example, absorption of workers in both public and private enterprises above some wage level may be determined by 'political quota'. Mobility may also be obstructed by family centered business not only in the tiny, informal and unorganized sector but also in organized production areas, as there is limited entry for 'outsiders' and often jobs in the high-wage occupations may be reserved for persons already in, or connected with the affluent society. Colonial heritage, wherein people educated in Western countries are preferred to people educated inside, may be a 'match-fixer'. The mobility of workers may also be constrained by non-innovative or stereotype jobs, wherein internal workers 'do the job'. Often the entry of individuals into the job market is 'time-tied', making workers' mobility non-operational for a stipulated period. Often highly qualified persons are obstructed from entering into middle level jobs and those below this level lest they leave the job at the very first opportunity because of their positive opportunity cost. Potential vertical mobility becomes a disqualification for such persons. Some type of entry may be delinked from any guarantee of jobs, such as Apprenticeship Schemes.

Some segmented entry and obstructions may occur in such an imperfect labour market. For example, for budding technologists and managers, often there is provision for 'campus recruitment' by established firms. This also depends on the credibility of the institution where these technologists and managers are being trained. In these institutions the per capita expenditure on education, either state-financed or private-financed, is much more than the social average expenditure on education per capita. The rate of return on education is also much higher for the persons coming out successfully from these institutions relative to the institutions that provide general skill. In a globalised economy, which is characterized by easy movement of skilled workers across countries, there occurs a drain of these technologists if the rate-differential is thought to be inadequate to stay in the 'home job'. The State-financed formation of manpower, thus, adds to the power of the countries outside the 'home country'.

(IV) Concluding Comments

Irrespective of the selection of a region, such as India as the selected economic unit while considering global mobility of labour, or a locality like a district within the national economy while considering workers' movement across alternative jobs, the task that has to be undertaken on a priority basis is the conversion of social categories into economic categories. In the context of labour, it means the conversion of caste division of labour into economic division of labour. This reveals both the inner weaknesses in a system and the need to re-orient the system. A low rate of unemployment, for example, may show the absence of structural change by occupation in an economy like India as also a declining level of living of population settled on land. It is, thus, imperative to test the technological advancement on land that will have effects on the working population that is dependent on land. This may lead to the displacement of a section of workers from land. If initial displacement is obstructed, the consequence may be trapping the increasing population, with probably a static percentage of the rising total population, to perpetual poverty. Only repenting over the hypothetical phenomenon of under-employment or disguised employment in agriculture, will lead to the prolonging of backwardness. A strong step towards exposing the problem, however, requires planning for rehabilitation of the workers in jobs that are based on and consistent with the knowledge base of these workers. The development of agriculture-related activities on an industrial basis, and development of local resource-based rural industries, etc., are the only routes whereby this population can be productively settled. The catalyst for these has to be the State.

References

Bhalla, G. S. (1995), "Globalisation and Agricultural Policy in India", *Indian Journal of Agricultural Economics*, Vol. 50, No. 1. January-March.

Census of India (1991), Registrar General and Census Commissioner India, Ministry of Home Affairs, *Primary Census Abstract, Series I, Part II-B(1)*, Vol. II. New Delhi.

DSHA (1998), Economics and Statistics Department, State Planning Institute, *District Statistical Handbook of Allahabad*, Uttar Pradesh.

Fern, Rober M. (1981), *Labour Economics: The Emerging Synthesis*, Winthrop Publication, Cambridge.

GOI (1991), *India's New Economic Policies*, Government of India, Ministry of External -----------Affairs, New Delhi.

ILO (1997-98), *World labour Report*, Geneva

————————(1998-99), *World Employment Report*, Geneva

————————(2000), *World Labour Report*, Geneva.

————————(2001), *World Employment Report*, Geneva

Majumder, Bhaskar (1995), "Manpower, Mobility in an Era of Globalization: Some Issues', *Productivity*, Vol. 36, No. 1, April-June.

——————————(1997), "Accommodating New Economic Policy in India's Social Dynamics: A Critical Review", *Productivity*, Vol. 37, No. 4, January-March.

——————————(2001), *Public Distribution System of Essential Commodities as a Social Safety Net: A Study of the District of Allahabad, Uttar Pradesh*, Report submitted to the Planning Commission, India.

National Institute of Rural Development (NIRD) (1999), *India Rural Development Report*, Hyderabad.

Reynolds, Lloyds (1951), *The Structure of Labour Market*, Harper & Brother, New York.

Rottenberg, S. (1968), "On Choice in Labour Markets", in McCormick, B.J. and Smith, Owen E.(eds), *The Labour Market*, Selected Readings, Penguin books.

6

Redundancy of Labour and Workers' Protection: An Analysis

Production in a functional sense implies combination of inputs with respect to time to produce a commodity. While commodity has a physical shape or volume, technology may be non-physical, like knowledge for doing a socially useful thing. Technology evolves as the necessity emerges. At any point of time there exists an accumulation of already evolved technologies. Commodity is the domain that gives expression to technology, while human labour and man-transformed resources (like machinery and equipment) are the means by which technology is expressed. Technology by itself is not quantified. What may be quantified are some of its indicators, like a particular technique of production, productivity of a particular input, expansion in production unit by size of quantified inputs, gestation period etc. This does not imply non-existence of the technologies that are yet to be understood and recorded.

As in conventional analysis, we assume two identifiable resources, labour and capital. For simplicity of analysis, we assume that labour-time applied on nature generates machinery; combined application of labour and machinery smoothens the transformation of nature into output. In this process, a section of the productive people previously called labourers now will be owners of machinery or may be seen now as owners of non-labour resources in addition to being owners of labour power. Hence, social division of labour gradually accommodates two sections of producers, one as owners of labour-cum-non-labour resources and the other as owners of only labour power. In fact, the initial commodity, which may be a machine, shows a crystallized form of labour of both these sections of producers and nature. However, once this distinction is accepted, we can write the production function as

$$Q = f(L, K),\ f_L > 0,\ f_{LL} < 0 \quad (1)$$

Q = Physical volume of output

L = Labour Time (hour) applied in producing Q

K = Machinery and equipment.

The geometric representation of (1) gives the total product curve. One such curve shows one state of technology, and shifting curves represent changing technologies. The commodity-technology association for the economy, thus, can be written as

$$(Q; T) = (Q_i, T_j) \quad (2)$$

Where Q is a vector of producible commodities, and T is a vector of technologies in production of Q.

$$Q = (Q_i),\ i = 1, 2, \ldots, n.$$

$$T = (T_j),\ j = 1, 2, \ldots, m. \quad (3)$$

where $m \geq n$, on the assumption of non-identical technology for any two commodities.

While alternative combinations of L and K show movement of a firm along a single total product (TP) curve, T is an operator that explains the shift of the TP curve. If a single product is considered, then technological improvement denotes improved ways of producing this product, i.e., the scale of production becomes higher, which potentially offers more efficiency (Hicks, 1971, p. 109).

Technological Progress and Labour Employment

We assume that (i) there are two firms, A_1 and A_2, who produce two commodities, Q_1 and Q_2. (ii) Each firm uses single non-identical technology, T_1 by A_1 and T_2 by A_2. The technologies (production function) follow a conventional neoclassical path. (iii) A_1 learns to improvise, so that for him technology shifts upward, expressed by an upward shift in total product curve. (iv) A_2 does not learn in parallel, so that for him technology curve remains unchanged.

We intend to examine the implications of this 'technological progress' on labour employment, and exit of the labourers, for A_1 and A_2, and for $(A_1 + A_2)$, that is, total economy.

Suppose, the initial state of technology, T_1, is known to the firm A_1 'by doing', so that the total product (TP) curve, Q_1 (T_1) is known to A_1. Each point on Q_1 (T_1) shows maximum possible output (Fig. 1) of the product Q_1, when A_1 uses least labour time (hour) $0L_0$, given full utilization of the capital stock that he possesses and given the technique of production (K/L) at $\tan\alpha$. For A_1, the level of output, thus, is determined at $0Q_1^0$. The relevant point on Q_1 (T_1) curve for A_1 is F, productivity of labour (AP_L) is tan γ and productivity of capital (AP_K) is $\tan\beta_1$.

Suppose, corresponding to a chosen technique of production, $\tan\alpha$, the previously employed labourers working for OL_0 labour-time invent improved methods of producing the same product, so that the TP curve shifts upward to $Q_1(T_3)$, T_3 being an improved technology. This means, with same L and same K/L, Q rises from

OQ_1^0 to OQ_1^1, AP_L rises from $\tan\Phi$ to $\tan\gamma$ and AP_K rises from $\tan\beta_1$ to $\tan\beta_2$.

Let ON be the portion of Q_1, required by A_1 for internal use (used for both consumption and intermediate purposes). The line NF_1 may be interpreted as real wages to support labourers inside the firm. For initial labour employment at OL_0, and output at OQ_1^0,

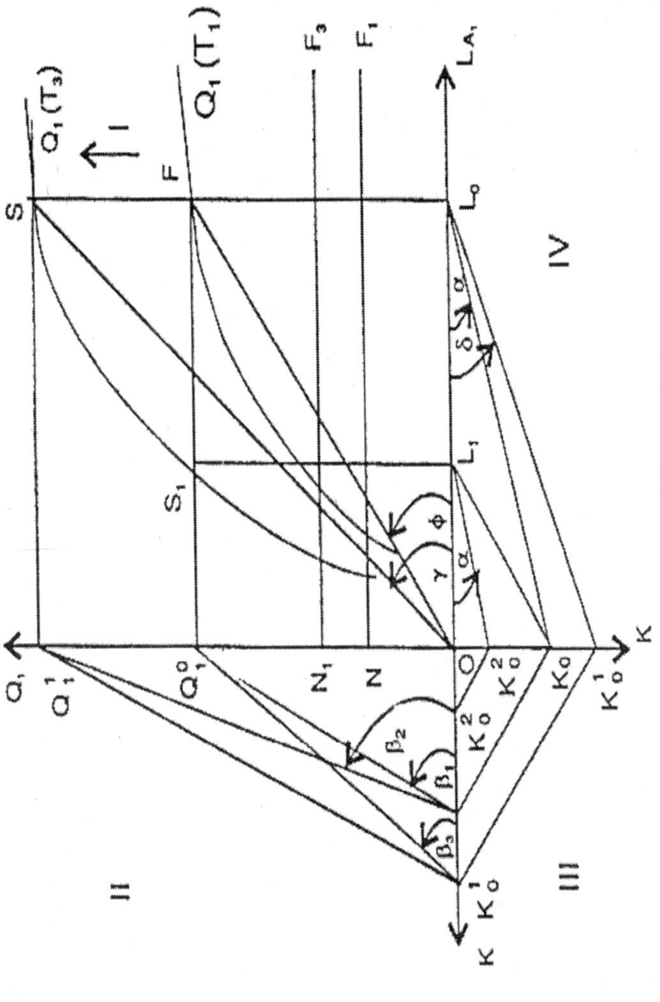

Fig. 1. (Firm A_1)

the surplus (over what is paid to labour) is NQ_1^0 that goes as return to capital used as OK_0.

Because of labour-led (knowledge, skill, training etc.) higher output for A_1 at OQ_1^1, surplus becomes NQ_1^1 i.e. rises by $Q_1^0Q_1^1$. Because of increased labour productivity at $\tan\gamma$ (associated with increased capital productivity at $\tan\beta_2$, curiously for same capital used), both the owners of labour-power and capital claim a higher share of $Q_1^0Q_1^1$. The real wage line for labour in A_1 thus shifts upward to N_1 F_3, $NN_1 < Q_1^0Q_1^1$, the gap ($Q_1^0Q_1^1$ - NN_1) goes as reward on capital used. One positive way for this gap to be utilized is outward (south-west) parallel shift of the K-stock (cum-use) line in quadrant-III to K_0 K_0. This raises K/L to tan δ if OK_0^1 is actually used and it leads to reduced capital productivity to $\tan\beta_3$. Reduced capital productivity may have implications like reduced rate of reward on capital (less than what corresponded to $\tan\beta_1$). If labour rate of reward remains unchanged at ON (correspond to higher labour productivity at $\tan\gamma$), then the initial gap $\left(Q_1^0Q_1^1 - NN_1\right)$ goes to capital owner, higher capital used multiplied by lower reward on capital per capita.

Let us consider now firm A_2, who produces Q_2. Given the state of technology T_2, the TP curve is Q_2 (T_2). For full utilization of the capital stock (OK_2) that A_2 possesses, labour employment by time (hour) is OL_2, given the technique of production at $\tan\Phi_1$. The quantity produced by A_2 is OQ_2^0, that the maximum A_2 can produce with determined labour employment and technique of production under the assumption of full utilization of capital stock (Fig. 2).

If OS is the real wage for labourers in A_2, then SQ_2^0 is the surplus for owners of non-labour (capital) resources. If A_1 and A_2 constitute the domain of production-cum-exchange and if all output is exchanged, then $NQ_1^0 \cong SQ_2^0$ shows the initial equivalence in exchange.

Now, following technological progress in A_1 and no technological progress in A_2, new exchange relation

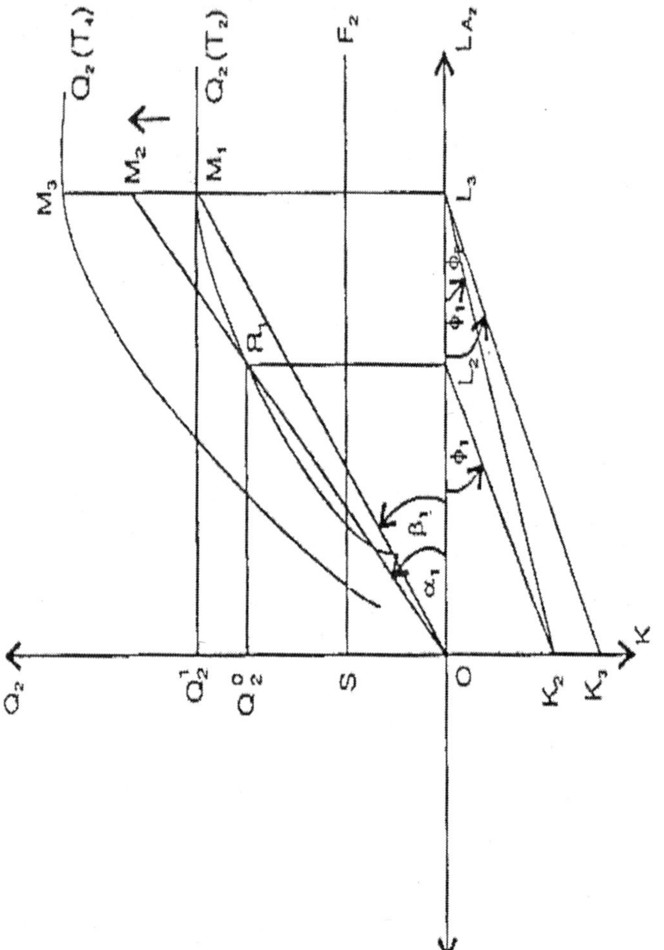

Fig. 2. (Firm A_2)

becomes $N_1Q_1^1 \cong SQ_2$, where $N_1Q_1^1 > NQ_1^0 \cong SQ_2^0$ so that the terms of trade for A_1 becomes adverse. Being the technology leader, A_1 can suppress this situation by restricting itself to point S_1 on Q_1 (T_3), whereby A_1 produces the initial output with less labour, OL_1. At S_1, the technique of production becomes more capital-intensive or less labour-intensive (Fig.1). If OL_0 labour employment is required for full utilization of capital at OK_0 then restricting labour employment to OL_1 means lesser-required capital and utilization, so that tan α is restored by capital employment at $K_0^2 \cdot K_0K_0^2$ capital thus remains un (under) utilized and labour exit from A_1 is L_0 L_1. With previous output, OQ_1^0, restored at S_1 on Q_1 (T_3) [west of F on Q_1 (T_1)], technological improvement for A_1 shows resource-saving.

What are the implications for A_2 and for the economy (A_1 + A_2)?

Suppose there is inter-firm labour mobility. Then L_0 L_1 labour (time contributed by labourers) shifts from A_1 to $A\varphi_2$. Suppose A_2 agrees to absorb it, labourers in A_1 being more productive. Thus, labour employment in A_2 becomes OL_3 (OL_2 by L_2 L_3 = L_0 L_1), so that even with reduced labour productivity $(\tan \alpha_1 > \tan \beta_1)$, total output increases to OQ_2^1 and surplus rises to $SQ_2^1 \left(> SQ_2^0\right)$. In the new situation, capital-labour ratio falls from $\tan \Phi_1$ to $\tan \Phi_2$. A capital stock of OK_2 needed OL_2 labour for full utilization of OK_2, given technique of production at $\tan \Phi_1$. Thus, OL_3 labour can only be absorbed if higher capital stock is generated at OK_3. This requires depressing real wage rate below OS in A_2, which is possible, when labour productivity has declined in A_2. The paradox is that absorption of L_2 L_3 labourers with past higher productivity (in A_1) leads to reduced labour productivity (along with initial labour OL_2) in A_2.

If either because of initial reaction to adverse terms of trade, or for resource-saving, A_1 comes back to producing OQ_1^0 output, generating initial surplus NQ_1^0, A_1 will be gainer, because NQ_1^0 will now be exchanged for $SQ_2^1 \left(SQ_2^0\right)$. A_2 with static technology that absorbs higher labour, thus, becomes a loser in exchange of commodities.

Either through wage depression (below OS) in A_2 or through import of capital from $A_1\left(=K_2K_3=K_0K_0^1\right)$, A_2 can move up the 'technology ladder' by combining increasing L and K. This will imply an upward shift of the TP curve, $Q_2(T_2)$ for A_2.

Even being a technology follower, one strategy of A_2, while absorbing additional labour from A_1, is to raise 'total labour productivity', thus, shifting the TP curve to $Q_2(T_4)$. This works when OL_2 and L_2L_3 (=L_0L_1 in Fig. 1) contribute towards raising productivity. The OR_1 line (ray), R_1 being the initial input-output combination on $Q_2(T_2)$, thus gets vertical push to M_3 above OR_1M_2, when OR_1M_2 shows $\tan\alpha_1$, that is, initial labour productivity. In other words, 'new labourer', rather than reducing 'combined labour productivity', raises labour productivity. Thus, for A_2 also there is a possibility of the TP curve getting an upward shift to $Q_2(T_4)$. To elaborate, the section of labourers that gets exit from A_1 contributed positively to 'combined enhancement of labour productivity' or 'technological improvement' in A_1. A section of labourers in A_1 who now move to A_2 get absorbed, may raise combined labour productivity in A_2. This may bring about similar situation in A_2 as experienced in A_1.

Redundancy of Labour and Scope for its Absorption

The labourers declared redundant in A_1 (measured via labour time, and not via identification of a section of labourers) by L_0L_1 gets the scope to be employed in A_2 (may be with a time lag) if A_2 agrees. On the supposition that all the labourers in A_1 contributed to technology shift, A_2 agrees on the assumption of fulfillment of 'new employment-led technological progress'. In practice, the accommodation of labourers that move from A_1 to A_2 may be a difficult task in A_2 because of a number of reasons. These include (i) capital constraint in A_2, where additional employment in A_2 is constrained by rigid per capita capital initially employed, (ii) established productivity-cum-wage linked labour hierarchy in A_2, limiting the scope for rearrangement of the established hierarchy,

(iii) In case of violation of (ii), a possibility of increasing intra-labour hierarchic differentiation in the domain of production in A_2, and hence non-cooperative production relation in A_2, (iv) the labourers initially employed in A_1 had particular skill (job-specific) which may not be reflected in A_2, (vi) A section of the labourers employed in A_2 may be willing to shift to A_1, because of higher real wage in A_1, which is, however, constrained by the particular skill required for absorption in A_1.

There is technological possibility for A_2 to move up the technology ladder. There is also the possibility for A_2 to get capital from A_1 (capital export by A_1 to A_2). There is also the organizational possibility for A_2 to depress the wage rate for labourers (initial plus new) in A_2, in case it moves along the initial total product (TP) curve, that is, raising output via employing more labour at reduced labour productivity. Suppose, then, A_2 declines to produce more via employing more labour (either on the initial TP curve or on a new shifted TP curve), for fear of facing adverse terms of trade vis-à-vis A_1. What happens to the economy, $(A_1 + A_2)$, in this situation? A_2 continues to produce OQ_2^0 and expects that the initial equivalence in exchange, or real terms of trade, will be restored. This terms of trade will be restored if A_1 chooses point S_1 on shifted technology curve $Q_1(T_3)$. This means A_1 will have to manage labour unemployment intra-A_1 by lessening working hours per labourer, i.e., offering more leisure without reducing real wage rate and without reducing the portion of Q_1 for internal use. A_1 cannot choose point F, because choosing F means surrendering the resource-saving benefits of technological progress.

Generally, the labourers at a low real wage rate prefer work to leisure. Thus, the choice of A_1 for reduction in per capita working hours per labourer is limited. Either A_1 moves up to point S or point S_1 or any point between S and S_1, all the points chosen are on new technology curve, $Q_1(T_3)$. Choosing S (which is rational for deriving the benefits of technological progress) means A_1 produces higher output at OQ_1^1. The additional output produced $Q_1^0Q_1^1$, will have two channels to be utilized: if A_1 does not (and since she can not, without making her real terms of trade adverse) export it to A_2 (and A_2 can not buy it at the same equivalence, given that her level of output remains unchanged with the same initial technology): (1) raising real wage rate, an upward parallel shift in NF_1 to N_1F_3, implying higher real wage corresponding to higher labour productivity, (2) capital formation, shown in quadrant III by an outward (south-west) movement, from K_0K_0 to $K_0^1K_0^1$. The magnitude of these shifts will depend on the relative power exercised by the controllers of capital and owners of labour power.

Example 1: Technology-led Redundancy of Workers

In Australia the largest steel producer is the Broken Hill Proprietary Company Limited (BPH). BPH has an integrated mill at Port Kembla that produces over 60.0 per cent of its output. Since the introduction of new technology associated with large investments on it, labour productivity has increased from 381 tonnes per employee per year in 1990 to 636 tonnes per employee per year in 1996. BHP also introduced 'team work' for quality improvement. What happened was a fall in employment at Port Kembla from 9,406 in 1990 to 7,036 in 1996. Unskilled iron workers were most adversely affected by redundancy and recruitment slowdown.

To counter redundancy as a problem, BHP developed up-skilling and career path advancement of iron workers. This career path incorporated both off-the-job training and on-the-job training and on-the-job competency testing. To supplement training, BHP developed adequate off-site training facilities in the region (ILO, 1998-99, p. 40).

Absence of technological progress for a firm means ultimate exit of the firm, while presence of technological progress leads to changing skill requirement, and hence obsolescence/redundancy of a section of workers previously employed in the firm. The initial labour employment was based on initial technology that included knowledge of the owners of labour-power and non-labour resources. Evolution of new knowledge leads to exit of owners of old knowledge. Pending a resolution on which type of knowledge is socially superior, the workers that face exit need protection for survival.

Social Protection of the Workers: Experience across Countries

Case 1: Developed Market Economies (DMEs)

The countries in the developed market economies (DMEs) have extensive unemployment insurance coverage and employment protection legislation that aim at employment security. These countries include Austria, Belgium, Denmark, Finland, France, Germany, Iceland, Luxembourg, Netherlands, Norway, Portugal, Spain, Sweden, and Switzerland. These countries offer for the working population high level and long duration unemployment insurance benefit payments. In contrast, within the DMEs, the duration of unemployment benefit payments is short, with benefits payable for less than twelve months, in countries like UK and US. The second layer of unemployment insurance, usually called unemployment assistance, that covers the unemployed workers who have exhausted their entitlement to unemployment insurance benefits, exists in countries such as Denmark, France, Spain and Sweden. In contrast, in Canada and the US, the unemployment benefit payments are not followed up with a second layer of unemployment assistance (ILO, 2000, pp. 148-149).

Employment protection legislation is strongly enforced in France, Germany and Spain. These are the countries where the most frequent cause of labour disputes arises from termination of employment contracts and judgments tend to be more favourable to employees. In Spain and Italy, labour court rulings seem to be favourable to workers because the beneficiary rate under unemployment insurance is lower than 20.0 per cent of the total of unemployed. The recent labour market reform in Germany strengthens the link between employment protection and unemployment insurance. In Germany, the amount of severance pay is partly taken into account in the calculation of the unemployment benefits, and particularly in part-time early retirement (ILO, 2000, p. 156).

In countries like Austria and Germany generous severance pay arrangements are increasingly transformed into job search and retaining plans for retrenched workers while they are still under contract with their previous employers (ILO, 2000, p. 156). The assumption is that execution of unemployment benefit schemes contributes to consumption smoothing and leaves people sufficient time to find a suitable job. In the DMEs, the calculation of unemployment benefits rests on the 'replacement level', that is, the benefit to be offered as a percentage of previous earnings and subject to the maximum period for which benefit is payable (ILO, 2000, p. 152-153). There are problems in execution of the benefit schemes. The reason is, employment protection is frequently dealt with in sectoral agreements between trade unions and employees or in enterprise-level collective agreements. This leaves the legislators with limited scope to influence overall trends in employment protection, especially in the already less-protected non-unionised segment of the labour force (ILO, 2000, pp. 155-156).

Case II: Central and Eastern European (CEE) Countries

The post-1989 countries in Central and Eastern Europe (CEE) established an employment fund that provided unemployment benefits and labour market support. This was a time when unemployment was still low in these countries. Average unemployment benefit replacement levels in the transition countries during post-1989 period seem comparable to those of the European Union. The replacement levels are calculated as a percentage of the worker's previous wage or of the average wage, but their maximum is usually not permitted to exceed a certain percentage of the national minimum wage. In post-1997 Hungary, maximum replacement levels could reach 75.0 per cent of the previous wage but could not exceed twice the value of the minimum wage. The rising and persistently high levels of unemployment in countries such as Bulgaria, Hungary, Poland, and Slovakia caused strains on unemployment benefit systems. This led to tighter eligibility rules, lower levels of replacement, shorter duration of benefits and lower beneficiary rates (ILO, 2000, pp. 157-158).

Immediately after 1989 many countries in CEE provided unemployment benefits for more than one year, but in the 1990s the length of duration often got reduced to three to six months. In Czech Republic, for example, unemployment benefits last for six months. In countries like Bulgaria, Lithuania, Poland, Slovakia, and Slovenia, the governments recognize the contribution of workers in building the country's wealth, and hence make short-term benefits policy more liberal by linking job seniority on the one hand and the duration and rate of benefits on the other (ILO, 2000, p. 158). In Croatia unemployment benefits are confined to a narrow range of low-level benefits.

In CEE countries, on an average, not more than half of the unemployed receive either unemployment benefits or social assistance. The percentage declined during the 1990s. During 1992-95 (January-December), the unemployment beneficiary rate declined from 80.0 percent to less than 40.0 percent in Hungary, from 75.0 percent to 55.0 percent in Poland, and from 82.0 percent 27.0 percent in Slovakia. In Poland only one-third of the registered unemployed have started receiving benefits of late (ILO, 2000, p. 158).

Case III: Developing Economies in Asia, Africa and Latin America

Latin America and the Caribbean: Countries in Latin America like Argentina, Barbados, Ecuador, Uruguay, and Venezuela have implemented unemployment insurance schemes, integrated within their social insurance schemes. In Brazil the unemployment insurance scheme is financed from a tax on enterprise revenues. In Chile this scheme is supported from general tax revenues. In Uruguay this scheme is supported from social insurance contributions and a part from value added tax. In Mexico the scheme is limited to workers between 60 and 64 years of age. The benefit entitlements to a worker depend in Mexico on the worker's contribution record. There are inter-country differentials in percentages of unemployed insurance benefits. For example, the proportion of unemployed persons receiving unemployment insurance benefits was 10.0 percent in Argentina, 16.0 per cent in Uruguay, both in December 1994, and 8.0 per cent in Chile as in 1993. For Barbados, the percentage of workers supported by unemployment insurance was 73.0 percent in 1986, which declined to 60.0 percent in 1994. Argentina and Chile pay unemployment benefits, which decline in steps, with duration of benefit ranging from four months to one year. Argentina, Brazil, Mexico, Peru and Uruguay introduced measures in the 1990s that aimed at devising or augmenting active labour market policies in an effort to deal with the problem of unemployment (ILO, 2000, pp. 159-160).

Asia

The countries in Asia in general do not care much for the need for unemployment protection legislation or unemployment insurance benefits. As late as in 1998 only four South-East Asian countries, namely, China, Mongolia, the Republic of Korea, and Hong Kong had any form of unemployment benefit scheme (ILO, 2000, p. 160-161). Unemployment insurance scheme in the Republic of Korea has been expanded in response to the massive rise in unemployment. The coverage of the unemployment benefit scheme in Korea was initially limited to firms with 30 or more workers. Since January 1, 1998, a planned extension of coverage to firms with ten or more workers was implemented and further to firms with five or more workers from March 1, 1998 (ILO, 2000, p. 162). In South Asia, only three countries, Bangladesh, India, and Pakistan have employer liability schemes to disburse severance or retrenchment payments on termination of employment.

Africa

We have not come across any country in Africa that has been practicing unemployment insurance benefits. Some of these countries have supporting employment and hence income-generating schemes. In eastern and southern Africa, ILO-supported employment-intensive programmes have been operating in Botswana, Kenya, the United Republic of Tanazania, and recently, in South Africa. Such schemes, however, are to be seen as measures for short-term protection of people, rather than any mechanism for substitution of unemployment insurance schemes.

Concluding Comments

Each firm in an economy is an optimizer of its own goal. Each firm tries to develop and move up the technology ladder, and thus, try to reap the benefits of higher productivity. This may lead to exit of a section of labourers from the firm that experiences technological improvement first. In a situation of practiced technological progress and derived technological gap, the inter-firm impact is felt by exercise of non-technology-led relative power of the participants, e.g., agreement/disagreement on joint benefits, sharing of real wages and sharing of products. Unless there comes a vent-for-surplus which may be thought of as a market (or autonomous demand) external for A_1 (the technology leader) where initial capital formation occurs, the options for expanding output with respect to technological improvement will not materialize. Thus, it may lead to: (i) possible exit of a section of labourers from the firm where they were initially employed, (ii) possible entry of this section of labourers into another firm, (iii) in absence of (ii), raising social costs of unemployment.

Technological progress leads to both additional employment and unemployment, depending on the changing skill required. The requirement is for both up-skilling and multi-skilling, both intra-firm and intra-firm. The organized industrial economies like the OECD countries, that experience technological progresses most, also cover most of the unemployed people as percentage of world total unemployed people. In countries like Austria and Germany, generous severance pay arrangements are increasingly transformed into job search and retraining plans for retrenched workers while they are still under contract with their previous employers (ILO, 2000, p. 156). The unemployment insurance benefits may also be used for investment in setting up a small business or to obtain training. Even the unused benefit entitlements of the unemployed workers may be used to subsidize enterprises, which hire these workers (ILO, 2000, p. 157).

In countries in the developing world, the problems are radically different from those experienced in the industrially developed countries. In the developing world, the size of the industrial sector is very small in terms of regular employment. These countries generally have underemployment, both in terms of productive man-days and the real wage rate. Hence, the kind of discussion that we made in the initial sections shows the realities in the industrially developed world as well as the possibilities in the developing world. This may show to the developing countries the necessity to protect the labourers prone to be technology-led redundant, as are their counterparts in the developed world. The small size of the existing labour force in the organized industrial sector is no excuse to bypass the issue.

References

Hicks, J. R. (1971), "The Social Framework", Oxford Univ. Press, London.

ILO, (1999), "World Employment Report", 1998-99, Bookwell, Delhi.

ILO, (2000), "World Labour Report", International Labour Office, Geneva.

7

Technological Progress and Redundancy of Workers: Tasks for Rehabilitation

(I) Introduction

It is established by now that the visible and explorable natural resources offer the individuals acting as economic agents the scope to produce commodities. Commodity is the concrete shape that any technology takes. Natural resources become visible and explorable also through technology. We concentrate in our analysis on technological progress and link it with labour employment, productivity etc. in the context of a national economy. The question of labour redundancy will be posed in the same context. We do not bring into analysis here movement of manpower across firms within the same national economy.

By workers, we mean the common sense view of the number of people in the working age. By employment, we consider here employment in the organized industrial sector. This includes both the workers in number and working hours per worker. In this paper, we assume that (1) production of a commodity is an engineering concept in the sense of converting inputs (man and matter) into output. This output includes products finally consumable by man and materials and machines useable by plants for further production. Thus, we include both final use and intermediate use of output. (2) The mode of production is capitalistic, in the sense of strict separation of economic agents in terms of distinctly revealed capacities as owners of labour and non-labour resources. (3) The capitalists pay wages (money and real) to the labourers in keeping with labour productivity. (4) Capitalists maximize surplus. (5) Adoption or application of technological progress in the domain of production is dependent on the owner of non-labour resources (the capitalist). We use the terms labour (number), workers, and manpower synonymously in this paper.

The paper is organized as follows. In Section II, we consider mutual impacts of technology and labour productivity on one another. In Section III, we consider the question of technological progress-led redundancy of labour. In Section IV, we raise the question regarding the vulnerability of workers when they are declared redundant. In Section V, we examine the question about the possibilities of rehabilitation of the workers declared redundant. Finally, in Section VI, we offer concluding comments.

(II) Technology and Manpower Productivity

In the standard literature on income, income-distribution, poverty (standard of living) etc., productivity of workers is cited as the root cause of a circle described as 'the vicious circle of poverty'. The arguments are offered from two sides of capital formation, the supply side and the demand side. On the supply side, there is the small capacity to save, resulting from the low level of real income. The low real income is a reflection of low productivity, which in its turn is due largely to the lack of capital. The lack of capital is a result of the small capacity to save, and so the circle is complete.

On the demand side, the inducement to invest may be low because of the small purchasing power of the people, which is due to their small real income, which again is due to low productivity. The low level of productivity, however, is a result of the small amount of capital used in production, which in its turn may be caused at least partly by the small inducement to invest (Nurkse, 1980, p. 5).

The task thus becomes breaking the vicious circle of poverty via raising productivity. The productivity question gets resolved to labour productivity by revealed choice of the owners of non-labour resources. How does it occur? Let us elaborate.

Let initial commodity production start at time point t_0. We assume equal access of individuals to natural resources at t_0. At time point t_1, some of the individuals will acquire more power (through possession of natural resources) to move ahead relative to others, because of application of superior technology. This superior technology may include application of physical force also, but essentially, it is superior brainpower developed via 'learning by doing'. The possession and application of superior technology leads to time-phased unequal command of individuals over non-labour resources. This also gives shape to sharp division of individuals as economic agents, particularly when the economy takes a capitalistic shape.

The higher the state of technology, the higher is the importance of non-labour resources (understood as lesser labour-time required for the old product being produced and not as lesser brain-intensity) and the lower is the importance of non-converted natural resources (like land in a gross sense). In fact, it is the worker who opens up the technological options.

We see technology as a way of combining quantified inputs into final output of a commodity. What is visible is not technology but the commodity that gives expression to technology. In concrete terms, human labour (number of workers engaged multiplied by man-hours applied) and man transformed resources (like machinery and equipment) are the means by which technology is expressed. In the literature there is theoretical support for such an approach (Hicks, 1971, p. 294). Thus, technology as such is not quantified, what is quantified are some its manifestations like a particular technique of production, productivity of a particular input, scale economies, gestation period etc.

In our simple frame of analysis we accept that labour time (hour) applied by labourers on nature (natural resources) generates machinery; labour and machinery, when combined, smoothen the transformation of nature into output (a product). In this process, a section of the productive people (workers) previously called labourers will now be owners of machinery or may be seen now as owners of non-labour resources. These owners of non-labour resources do not automatically shed their labour power, nor can they. What they do is to take the opportunity of applying non-labour power and legitimize high and higher returns on non-labour power. This is where the application of social division of labour takes a sharp turn - from pre-capitalist mode to capitalist mode. Social division of labour in a time phasing manner accommodates two groups of producers, one as owners of labour-cum-non-labour resources and the other as owners of only labour power. Once this distinction is accepted, and applied for appropriate relative shares from output produced, the relation between productive forces takes a definite shape as

$$Q = f(L, K), f_L > 0, f_{LL} < 0 \qquad \text{........1}$$

Where Q denotes physical volume of output of a commodity,
L denotes labour time (hour) applied in producing Q,
K denotes machinery and equipment,
f denotes technology.

'f' gets manifested in terms of technique of production (K/L), input productivity (Q/L, Q/K), and scale economies, that is,

$$(\lambda L, \lambda K) \rightarrow \lambda^n Q, \gtreqless 1, \lambda \geq 0$$

The geometric representation of equation (1) is known as the total product curve on the input (variable) –output space, one curve representing one state of technology (T), and shifting curves representing changing technologies. Technologies (T) thus denote the nature of association between human labour and non-human resources. While a conventional production function explains the movement of Q along a single product curve, T is an operator that explains the shift of the curve.

(III) Technological Progress and Redundancy of Workers

Let us consider a single product that is being produced by a firm (economy) whose physical volume is denoted by Q. Technological improvement then implies improved ways of producing Q with respect to at least one variable factor. If all the factors (K, L) are made variables by λ ratio $(\lambda \geq 0)$, then there is a scale effect. We concentrate on the case where

$K = K_0$ (fixed).

Then improved technology means an upward shift in total product curve (Q) for a specified labour (by number or hour) employed.

Let the initial state of technology, T_1, be known to the firm, represented by the total product curve, $Q(T_1)$, each point on which shows maximum possible output of the single product (Fig. 1).

For full utilization of K at K_0, if the required labour employment L_0 is actually employed by the firm (owner of capital), then at a pre-specified capital-labour ratio (K/L) at $\tan\alpha$, Q is determined at Q_0, labour employment being L_0. The productivities of inputs are shown by $\tan\beta$ as average product of labour (AP_L) and $\tan\gamma$ as average product of capital (AP_K).

We consider a situation where corresponding to chosen technique of production at $\tan\alpha$, the employed workforce invents improved methods of producing the same product, so that now there is a non-parallel upward shift in total product curve to $Q(T_2)$, T_2 representing improved state of technology. This means that with same L and same K/L, Q rises from OQ_0 to OQ_1, AP_L rises from $\tan\beta$ to $\tan\theta$, and AP_K rises from $\tan\lambda$ to $\tan\phi$. If OL_0 labour is accommodated by capital (firm), it will imply higher command of both the owners of capital and labour over the commodity produced.

Now suppose Q_0Q_1, in totality or a part of it, can not be sold (or is not sold by the capital owner) in the market. This would imply that on the newly established $Q(T_2)$ curve, the capital owner would prefer a point anywhere between F and G. Any southwest movement on FG would imply labour redundancy, and higher capital intensity. A point like G on $Q(T_2)$ would imply higher labour productivity, same capital productivity, lower labour employment, and higher capital-labour ratio. The paradox thus is that higher labour productivity leads to labour redundancy. The paradox may be resolved once the constraints (real or imposed) are taken into account, namely, market size or aspiration of capital accumulation at the cost of labour.

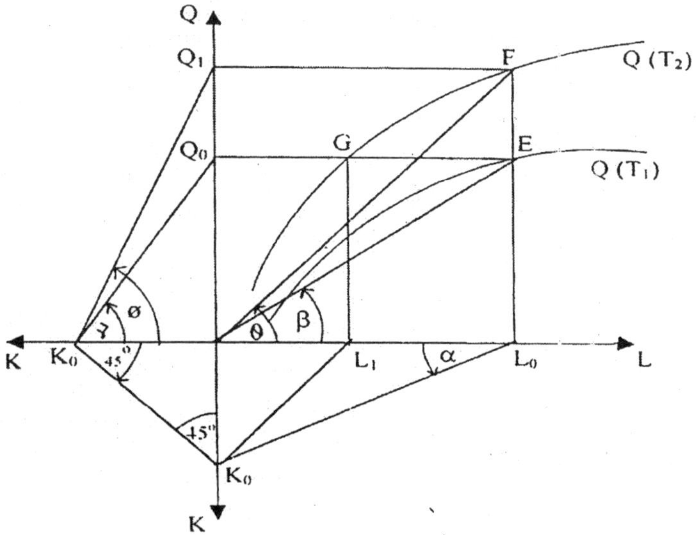

Figure 1

In reality, the point G on Q (T_2) is likely to be transitory, once it is understood that initial labour employed at OL_0 as a whole contributed to an upward shift of Q curve from $Q(T_1)$ to $Q(T_2)$ and not any segment of OL_0. Once thus L_0 L_1 labour is declared redundant, it will have further adverse impact on size of market, unless the wage rate (and wage bill) for OL_1 labour can compensate for the wage rate (and wage bill) of OL_0 labour employment. The implicit assumption is that the wage bill (most of it) understood by the cardinal indicator of consumption propensity goes to be spent in the market (demand).

The implication is that technological improvement-led labour redundancy is labour (knowledge) made, while capital takes advantage of it by non-realization (non-marketing) of higher volume of output produced. Thus, capital-ownership, via market constraint or capital accumulation, shows redundancy of labour. The controllers of capital offer the workers the option for 'voluntary retirement' from the concerned firm. The objective basis is that lesser number of workers, with same labour hour per head, will be producing initial output or more. Generally, the controllers of capital will seek higher output so that the whole of L_0L_1 labour will not be displaced. The objective of the controllers of capital to seek output higher than OQ_0 may be attempted for a number of reasons, which we do not spell out here. The apparently easy solution in terms of maintaining a balance between output and labour employment by elimination (exit) of a section of workers can not solve the problem on the medium and long-term. This is because such a short-term solution would accentuate market constraint. Also, it may be difficult to identify that section of workers who are redundant since all the previously employed workers contributed positively towards coordinated action in the output space and technological improvement. Whatever we have told so far rests on labour-led technological improvement.

Let us consider a second situation where two products (or, n products, $n > 2$) are produced (and used) in an interdependent way. We assume no prior information to any of the firms producing these products about technological improvement in the other firm(s). As a concrete case, we take the case of firms producing pen (writing), ink (used for pouring inside the pen) and blotting paper (used to soak ink on the writing paper). Technological improvement in the firm that produces pen may lead to ultimate non-use of ink and hence exit of blotting paper. By implication, workers previously engaged in ink, and blotting paper manufacturing firms, will have to face redundancy or exit. This redundancy is delinked from technological improvement, if any, in the concerned products (ink, blotting paper) where the workers were previously safely employed. Here, the substitution in use of a product (of a variety) A (say, pen) leads to exit of products B (ink) and C (blotting paper). The redundancy in labour could also come in product A (pen) whose end-use pattern changed by technological change. This we considered in the previous case (Fig. 1). What we stress here is unforeseen (in absence of prior information) but abruptly declared redundancy of labour by controllers of technology (firm).

Now suppose the third situation. Let there be prior information about technological change, within the firm and for the interdependent firms. Within the firm it may be knowledge-based in the sense of evolution of improved ways of producing the same product. In the context of interdependent firms, it is adoption of improved techniques developed in some other firm directly relevant for a product different from what the concerned firm is producing but affecting the learning process of the concerned firm. Be it intra or inter-firm, the technology becomes time-saving for producing the same volume of output in the concerned firm, and hence will have a tendency to reduce the size of the workforce. The workers come to know at a certain date that they are going to be declared redundant. What do they do?

(IV) Displacement/Exit of Workers when they are Declared Redundant

We assume that a worker joins a job independent of his own choice and often in conditions of ignorance. He acquires some general skill (knowledge) and some particular skill. This knowledge is primarily linked with how to get a job done, given freedom (time, materials and machines, favourable environment) to the worker. The alienation of the potential worker (job seeker) from most of the required freedom in a capitalist mode of production always keeps him as a potential victim. The firm-specific potential victimization could be overcome by being mobile across firms. This is however conditioned by acquiring multiple skills. In addition, the corporate attachment of community culture within the particular firm where the concerned workers are initially absorbed may obstruct any mobility of this workforce. From the viewpoint of the particular firm, such an attachment of the workforce is not criticized up to a point. The emergence of market constraint for the firm producing a single product after that critical point of time shows a mature stage of production where labour employment comes to be criticized. This criticism is really an objective evaluation of the performance of the workforce, measured not only by labour productivity but also profitability of the firm. The consequence is that less than any hypothetical minimum profit leads to questioning the size of the labour force in the existing firm. We explain the emergence of this mature stage of production for the firm by technological improvement. This technological improvement is essentially knowledge-based, where knowledge gets reflected in time-saving communication (information), capital-use etc. The gap is required knowledge at a mature stage of production and the knowledge that was required at the entry point of the concerned worker in the past is the reason behind displacement/exit of the worker.

Even if the workers are willing to be mobile across firms, their knowledge of wage and non-wage terms of employment in other jobs is limited. If we assume that the workers are aware of the existence of the wage-differential in similar jobs for which they seem to be employable, then it makes sense that, *ceteris paribus*, labour mobility will be a direct function of wage-differential. If the labour market is perfectly competitive, then the workers are rational optimizers. In practice, the labour mobility, if any, is wage-insensitive and there arise non-wage factors and forces to cause immobility of workers. These non-wage factors and forces are often non-economic also, for example, factors like language, culture, etc.

Underdeveloped economies in general are characterized by immobility of workers. This is because they do not have information about better job opportunities elsewhere, if job opportunities exist at all, or because they are unable to move and offer their job skill today here and tomorrow there. Labour mobility as such is conditioned at the beginning by additional job opportunities, and subsequently conditioned by wage flexibility and wage-differential, probability of getting a job elsewhere, linguistic-cultural-accommodative factors in the regions offering job opportunities etc. With no additional labour absorption in the national economy, there may occur intra-and inter-sectoral reallocation of labour. However, in a state of increasing population, it would imply increasing unemployment. Thus, effective labour mobility also requires increasing job opportunities across firms.

Institutional Rigidities: Example of India's Labour Market

Mixed capitalist economies like India are subject to state control via economic planning. The industrial system has evolved here in such a way as to make the establishments 'internally closed'. This allows entry into the establishments at the lowest level or provides limited entry points at the middle and upper levels. Most of the positions in the establishments are filled through internal promotions, offering little opportunities for competition. Thus, there exist institutional-cum-administrative barriers to entry and mobility of labourers across both public and private sectors within such mixed economies. As labour mobility requires execution of additional responsibilities (like housing etc.) by the establishments, it is generally discouraged. In underdeveloped economies in particular, non-contractual, productivity-neutral labour employment based on provision for time-scale salary and seniority-based promotion leads to offer the individual employed in the same firm higher designation and probably higher degradation. This is not to imply that the quality degradation of a worker is a direct function of maturity by age. What we imply here is the workers' reluctance to move from low wage certainty in the existing firm to high wage uncertainty in a different firm. This rigidity in labour market is sector-neutral and plant-neutral. It is essentially rooted in socio-political-institutional-cultural set up of the country.

Often inter-industrial mobility of workers is constrained by imposition of political (in) discipline, for example, in terms of absorption of workers in enterprises. This absorption above some wage category is determined by 'political quota'. The industrial establishments often resemble family-centered business, where not only in tiny, informal and unorganized sector but also in organized industrial plants, there is limited entry for 'outsiders'. Often jobs in the high wage occupations or responsible positions are reserved for persons in, or connected with, the affluent society. The country in question may have colonial heritage, where people educated abroad are preferred to people educated inside the country. The job pattern in the existing establishments may be non-innovative or stereotype, where internal workforce is preferred to external ones. Often the nature of entry into the job market is time-tied, making mobility of the workforce non-operational for the stipulated period. Many of such situations are beyond the control of the workforce, either in seeking jobs or in changing jobs.

Technological-cum-Organizational Barriers in Labour Absorption: Evidences from Some Third World Countries

In addition to all the above, industrialization brings with it a movement from lower-order technology to higher-order technology. On this technology trajectory, the workforce may become prone to self-destruction. This is self-destruction because, as we argued in the beginning, a section of the advanced learners in jobs brought about this trajectory. During the 1990s in the Indian industrial sector, as high as 30.0 per cent redundancy was estimated in the organized sector employing around 28 million. The 243 operating Central Public Enterprises alone shed 200,000 jobs during 1991-97 through means other than retrenchment. In addition, as high as 15,534 workers were retrenched in organized industrial sector during 1992-97. The Steel Authority of India reduced its work force from 2,30,000 in 1986 to 1,80,000 in 1997. In Indian Railways it has already been estimated that as high as 33.0 per cent of the workforce is redundant. The Tata Iron and Steel Co. in the private sector have planned recently to downsize its workforce to one-third of its present size (Venkata Ratnam, 1998, p. 376-377). Across countries in the world, as many traditional production functions are displaced by machines, there has been a fall in employment of production workers. This has been accompanied by a redefining of much production work, as the introduction of new technology and new forms of work organization (which tend to complement IT) requires production workers to be more skilled and knowledgeable (ILO, 1999, p. 39). Because of pervasive IT effects in industries and workplace, the newly unskilled workers are declared redundant. There has come job destruction along with job creation. The Broken Hill Proprietary Company Limited (BHP), the largest steel producer in Australia, shed its workforce from 9406 in 1990 to 7036 in 1996. The victims were the unskilled ironworkers. The reduction in size of the workforce came along with "up-skilling and career path development for ironworkers who used to acquire skills traditionally (mainly developed on the job) without formal training" (ILO, 1999, p. 40).

In Latin American countries, the demand for unskilled labour has fallen significantly during 1990s. As is true in general for all economies in their respective stages of development, dual labour market has evolved as a consequence of skill-specific displacement from organized formal to unorganized informal sector. The declining demand for labour in the former also weakens the wage-status of the workers in the latter, the workers in the latter called 'unskilled' with respect to technological improvement in the former. In addition to technological improvement for raising manpower productivity, leading to displacement of manpower by declared redundancy, the same consequence may be seen from restructuring the public sector as in India of 1990s and the entry of many of these economies in global competitive network.

Argentina in Latin America provides an example where accelerating economic growth during 1990s by 5.8 per cent following imposition of structural adjustment programme led to deteriorating employment scenario. Between 1991 and 1995 the rate of unemployment increased from 6.3 per cent to a maximum of 17.5 per cent in 1995, and settled at 15.0 per cent in 1997.

Public sector employment fell from 19.3 per cent of total employment in 1990 to just 13.2 per cent in 1996 (ILO, 1999, pp. 20-21).

The general downsizing of the workforce thus may rest on the following factors:

- Changed product mix and the rapid disappearance of the requirement for traditional skills.
- Changing location of production and obstructed mobility of workers.
- Non-renewal of previously acquired specialization by workers.
- Abrupt effort by the owners of non-labour resources to accommodate the entry of transnational capital in the firm.
- Managerial inefficiency in diversification of products to compensate the probable contraction in market faced by the firm.
- Managerial apathy towards R&D and training for skill formation of workers.
- Application of capital-deepening technical progress.
- Downsizing of less efficient workers on the basis of intra-firm efficiency parameters accepted by the owners of non-labour resources.

At the operational level, the downsizing of workers declared redundant occurs by withdrawal of state support to loss-making Public Sector Enterprises (PSEs), closure of industrial units (both in public and private) declared sick, privatization of PSEs and hence adoption of hire and fire methods by managers in private enterprises (Chandra, 1999 p. 32; Alam and Mishra, 1998, p. 279). The downsizing of the workforce is resorted not because of absolute inter-temporal reduction in productivity per worker. The scope for downsizing may crop up from relative productivity. The changes in technology and work organization, often complementing each other, have resulted in a shift in the nature of skill demand. The changing character of new technologies requires workers who can learn and adapt to these changes quickly and efficiently. Though the skill itself may not be higher, the ability to master it quickly and use it productively calls for a high level of confidence and familiarity that favours the higher skilled' (ILO, 1999, p. 46). The relative obsolescence and degradation of a section of the workforce is manifested when there emerges a relatively advanced section of the manpower within the firm or even outside. The relatively advanced section contributes significantly towards inventions and innovations. While adoption of this 'new knowledge' by the firm makes some labourers vulnerable in terms of continuing with initial job-specifications, the chance of entry of this advanced section in a fully operated (optimal capacity) firm will have a tendency to crowd out the section relatively less advanced. The latter section by consequence is declared redundant at the level of the firm.

There has to be a method to offer the workers an avenue to resettle once redundancy is declared for the workers identified. One such avenue being practiced in Indian industries is offering the monetary benefits from the Voluntary Retirement Scheme (VRS) to the workers. In its attempt to realize maximum (output) benefits from 'learning effect' the enterprises may plan rationalization of its workforce by offering VRS. The difficulty in the execution of such a scheme is that the more efficient (by learning) workers at the middle age (median age by service span generally understood) may opt for such VRS, while the less efficient workers stay. This is because for the former it works as a money supporting device for vertical (or at least horizontal) mobility, while for the latter safety remains by non-opting for VRS. This is likely to have reflections on the quality of the product, state of technology and work environment inside the plant that opted for and executed VRS (Rameshan, 1998, p. 107). The general frame that we conceived at the beginning remains undisturbed, namely, workforce-led technological improvement and technology-led exit of workforce. This technology-determined exit of a section of the workforce has to be rehabilitated to socially useful old technology-based jobs. This is, however, constrained by the efforts of the people without economic jobs for entry.

(V) Tasks for Rehabilitation

The question of rehabilitation is an economic question in addition to being an ethical as well as a social question. It is an ethical question because the initial competence of a worker for inclusion in a plant cannot at ease wither away because of inter-temporal relative (inter-personal) less competence. It is a social question because the service rendered so far by the workers inside a plant was very much based on social co-operation. In other words, attainment of the initial PPC was very much a reflection of co-operation among workers at all layers inside the plant. The question is economic because the size of market is contracted by long term displacement of workers. The implicit assumption is that the wage base of the residue workers cannot compensate for the wage bill now being truncated because of labour displacement. The issue is not a hypothetical conflict between new employment of more efficient workers (from the viewpoint of technology and capital), but is a question of assuring the initially employed workers a notion of safety by wage-income and work opportunity inside the plant. There is no reason to delink wage-income from work-productivity. Rehabilitation of a section of the currently employed workforce is a relevant question if the section can be identified. To counter obsolescence and to ensure rehabilitation, we suggest the following measures:

- Ensuring both general and particular skill at the level of the plant as soon as the individual is absorbed.
- Implementing job rotation programmes inside a plant.
- Ensuring continuous training for the workforce inside plants to offset both deterioration and obsolescence.

- Counseling for workers to understand their perceptions about the job, their attitude to work etc.
- Ensuring not only on the job training, but also on the job competency test based on training.
- Making people inside the plant understand the complementarity between machine and man.
- Developing responsible trade unionism for understanding the initial labour displacing effect of the machine.
- Ensuring on-site and off-site training, particularly for those workers who face exit by rationalization of the plant in response to high-tech industrialization.
- Income-support for conducting training programmes for workers.
- Developing or adopting diversified products by the advanced section of the workforce so that the existing workforce can be reallocated.
- Promoting sunrise industries in case some products belong to sunset enterprises.

Training is a major exercise to keep workers on the job where they were employed years ago (ILO, 1999, p. 187). There is, however, no alternative to generating the scope for labour employment by selection of appropriate products and technologies. There is enough scope for labour-based and local resource-based technologies that offer increasing scope for employment generation. The examples may include both productive physical infrastructure and social infrastructure. The first category includes land reclamation, minor dams, irrigation systems, drainage, link roads, canals etc., while the second one includes schools at multi-levels and health centers. Rehabilitation of workers declared redundant thus is not only a function of training of workers, but also a function of selection of labour absorbing products/plants/ sectors. Market alone may show sometimes wrong signal, particularly when the rehabilitation question of the handicapped workers (by birth or on the job) is considered. There may arise the need for providing employment subsidy here.

(VI) Concluding Comments

Resistance to technological change will be much less if the workers have the confidence in the ability of the entrepreneurs, including the Government, to provide alternative jobs. To be brief, the workers join jobs independent of their own will. The technology applied is not within the jurisdiction of the workers, though present machines are the products of the past workers engaged in the same or in a different plant. But the present use of that machine is not within the discretion of the workers engaged at present nor could the past workers deny production of the machines produced in the past and used at present. The capital that goes to buy or hire machine and labour hour is independent of the choice of the workers. The obsolescence of a section of the workers is dependent on introduction of new technology and hence time-dependent. The inherent inequality in brainpower will bring about technology-led redundancy of a section of the workforce. By absolute productivity, this section may justify their wage rate being received. The inter-temporal productivity of this section declared redundant might have also increased to justify enhanced wage rate. Nevertheless, this section declared redundant could not escape relative deterioration in terms of productivity, that is, relative to the more advanced section. A section of the workforce at best can try to delay the process of their own obsolescence but cannot stop it. This section of the workforce becomes more vulnerable if they were in plants that are now sunset. A plant becomes a sunset plant at a stage of production because of factors beyond the control of the workers employed at present. The factors that determine whether a plant will be sunset will depend on ownership and control of capital, technology and rationalization of the plant. If the plant is rationalized, by which we mean downsizing manpower, then the section that is victimized is the displaced workforce. The assumption is that the rationalization is labour saving. There is the threat that if the firm does not initiate rationalization, there emerges the problem of the exit of the plant itself. The task is to establish sunrise plants, plan localization of plants appropriate for existing skill of the displaced workforce, ensuring new employment of the workers displaced from sunset plants and plants set for rationalization. The tasks rest on the workers at multi-layers in a plant (acquiring skill by job rotation, for example), the managers in a plant (by diversification of products and technological choice), and the extra-plant authority (for example, the institutions and the state by actions and policies).

References

Alam, Moneer and Mishra, S. N., (1998), 'Structural Reforms and Employment Issues in India: A Case of Industrial Labour', *The Indian Journal of Labour Economics*, Vol. 41, No. 2, April-June.

Chandra, Ashok, (1999), 'Retraining for Redevelopment: NRF Initiative and Challenge in Training', *The Indian Journal of Labour Economics*, Vol. 42, No. 1, Jan-March.

Hicks, J. R., (1971), *The Social Framework*, London, Oxford Univ. Press.

International Labour Office (1999), *World Employment Report*, 1998-99.

Nurkse, R. (1980), *Problems of Capital Formation in Under-developed Countries*, Oxford, Basil Blackwell.

Rameshan, P., (1998), 'Employment Reduction under Reforms and the Productivity of sick PSEs: A Learning Curve Analysis', *The Indian Journal of Labour Economics*, Vol. 41, No. 1, Jan-March.

Venkata Ratnam, C. S., (1998), 'Economic Reforms and Labour', *Productivity*, V. 39, No. 3, Oct-Dec.

8

Technological Progress, Redundancy and Rehabilitation of Workers: A Theoretical Note

(I) Introduction

Production-centered economic analysis is at the center of analyses in economics. It is established by now that the visible and explorable natural resources offer the individuals acting as economic agents the scope to maximize output per period. On a commodity space, it is a north-east movement to attain the production possibility curve (PPC) or frontier. Commodity is the concrete shape that the technology takes. Natural resources become visible and are also explorable through technology. We concentrate in our analysis on technology and technological progress and link these with labour employment, productivity, etc. The question of labour redundancy will be posed in the same context.

By workers, we mean the common sense view of the number of people in the working age. By employment, we consider the labour employment in the organized industrial sector. This includes both the workers and the number of working hours per worker. In this paper, we assume that (a) production of a commodity is an engineering concept in the sense of converting inputs (man and matter) into output. This output includes products finally consumable by man and materials and machines usable by plants for further production. Thus, we include both final use and intermediate use of output; (b) the mode of production is capitalistic, in the sense of strict separation of economic agents in terms of distinctly revealed capacities as owners of labour and non-labour resources; (c) the capitalists pay wages (money or real) to the labourers in keeping with labour productivity; (d) capitalists maximize surplus; (e) adoption or application of technological progress in the domain of production is dependent on the owner of non-labour resources (the capitalist). We use the terms labour (number) and workers synonymously in this paper.

This paper has five sections. In Section I we consider mutual impact of technology and labour productivity on one another. In Section II we consider the question of technological progress-led redundancy of labour. In Section III we raise the question regarding the vulnerability of workers when they are declared redundant. In Section IV we examine the question about the possibilities of rehabilitation of the workers declared redundant. Finally, in Section V we offer concluding comments.

(II) Technology and Labour Productivity

In the literature on income, income-distribution, poverty (standard of living), etc. productivity of workers is cited as the root cause of a circle described as 'the vicious circle of poverty'. The arguments are offered from two sides of capital formation. Let us see some arguments. On the supply side, there is little capacity to save, resulting from the low level of real income. The low real income is a reflection of low productivity which, in turn, is largely due to the lack of capital. The lack of capital is a result of little capacity to save, and so the circle is complete. On the demand side, the inducement to invest may be low because of the insignificant purchasing power of the people, which is due to their small real income, which again is due to low productivity. The low level of productivity, however, is a result of the small amount of capital used in production, which in its turn may be caused, at least partly, by little inducement to invest (Nurkse, 1980, p. 5).

The task thus becomes breaking the vicious circle of poverty by raising productivity. The productivity question gets resolved due to labour productivity by revealed choice of the owners of non-labour resources. How does it occur? Let us elaborate.

Let initial commodity production start at time point t_0. We assume equal access of individuals to natural resources at t_0. At time point t_1 some of the individuals will acquire more power (through possession of natural resources) to move ahead relative to others, because of application of physical force also, but essentially it is superior brainpower developed via 'learning by doing'. The possession and application of superior technology leads to time-phased unequal command of individuals over non-labour resources. This also gives shape to sharp division of individuals as economic agents particularly when the economy takes a capitalistic shape.

The higher the state of technology, the higher is the importance of non-labour resources (understood as lesser time required for the old product being produced and not as lesser brain-intensity) and the lower is the importance of non-converted natural resources (like land in a gross sense). In fact, it is the worker who opens up the technological options.

We see technology as a way of combining quantified inputs into final output of a commodity. What is visible is not technology, but the commodity that gives expression to technology. In concrete terms, human labour (number of workers engaged multiplied by man-hours applied) and man-transformed resources (like machinery and equipment) are the means by which technology is expressed. In the literature there is theoretical support for such an approach (Hicks, 1971, p. 294). Thus, technology as such is not quantified — what is quantified are some of its manifestations like a particular technique of production, productivity of a particular input, scale economies, gestation period, etc.

In our simple frame of analysis we accept that labour time (hour) applied by labourers on nature (natural resources) generates machinery; labour and machinery, when combined, smoothen the transformation of nature into output (a product). In this process, a section of the productive people (workers) previously called labourers will now be owners of machinery or may be seen now as owners of non-labour resources. These owners of non-labour resources do not automatically shed their labour power nor can they. What they do is, take the privilege of applying non-labour power and legitimize high and higher returns on non-labour resources. This is where the application of social division of labour takes a sharp turn from pre-capitalist mode to capitalist mode. Social division of labour in a time phasing manner accommodates two groups of producers, one as owners of labour-cum-non-labour resources and the other as owners of only labour power. Once this distinction is accepted, and applied for appropriate relative shares from output produced, the relation between productive forces takes a definite shape as

$$Q = f(L, K), f_L > 0, f_{LL} < 0 \qquad \text{...............(1)}$$

Where Q denotes physical volume of output;
L denotes labour time (hour) applied in producing Q;
K denotes machinery and equipment;
f denotes technology.

'f' gets manifested in terms of technique of production (K/L), input-productivity (Q/L, Q/K), and scale economies, that is, $(\lambda L, \lambda K) \rightarrow \lambda^n Q, \gtreqless 1, \lambda \geq 0$

The geometric representation of equation (1) is known as the total product curve on the input (variable) — output space, one curve representing one state of technology (T), and shifting curves representing changing technologies. Technology (T) thus denotes the nature of association between human labour and non-human resources. While a conventional production function explains the movement of Q along a single product curve, T is an operator that explains the shift of the curve.

(III) Technological Progress and Redundancy of Workers

Let us consider a single product that is being produced by a firm (economy) whose physical volume is denoted by Q. Technological improvement then implies improved ways of producing Q, with respect to at least one variable factor. If all the factors (K, L) are made variables by λ ratio $(\lambda \geq 0)$, then there is a scale effect. We concentrate on the case where $K=K_0$ (fixed).

Then improved technology means an upward shift in total product curve (Q) for a specified labour (by number or hour) employed.

Let the initial state of technology, T_1, be known to the firm, and represented by the total product curve, Q (T_1), each point on which shows maximum possible output of the single product (Fig. 1).

For full utilization of K at K_0, if the required labour employment L_0 is actually employed by the firm (owner of capital), then at a pre-specified capital-labour ratio (K/L) at $\tan\alpha$, Q is determined at Q_0, labour employment being L_0. The productivities of inputs are shown by $\tan\beta$ as average product of labour (AP_L) and $\tan\gamma$ as average product of capital (AP_K).

We consider a situation where corresponding to a chosen technique of production at $\tan\alpha$, the employed workforce invents improved methods of producing the same product, so that now there is non-parallel upward shift in total product curve to $Q(T_2)$, T_2 representing improved state of technology. This means that with same L and same K/L, Q rises from OQ_0 to OQ_1, AP_L rises from $\tan\beta$ to $\tan\theta$, and AP_K rises from $\tan\gamma$ to $\tan\phi$. If OL_0 labour is accommodated by capital (firm), it will imply higher command of both the owners of capital and labour over the commodity produced.

Now suppose, Q_0Q_1, in totality or a part of it, cannot be sold (or is not sold by the capital owner) in the market. This would imply that on the newly established $Q(T_2)$ curve, the capital owner would prefer a point anywhere between F and G. Any south-west

Figure 1

Total Product Curve

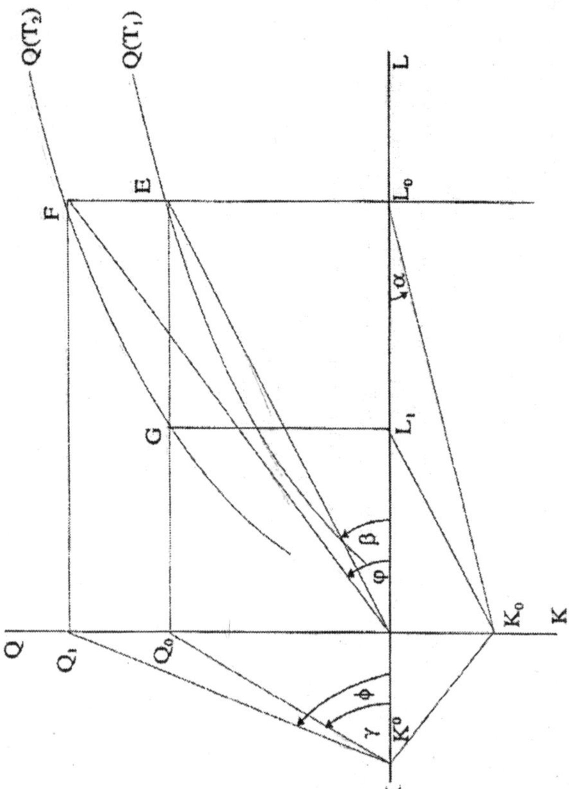

movement on FG would imply labour redundancy, and higher capital intensity. A point like G on $Q(T_2)$ would imply higher labour productivity, same capital productivity, lower labour employment, and higher capital-labour ratio. The paradox thus is that higher labour productivity leads to labour redundancy. The paradox may be resolved once the constraints (real or imposed) are taken into account, namely, market size or aspiration of capital accumulation at the cost of labour.

In reality, the point G on $Q(T_2)$ is likely to be transitory, once it is understood that initial labour employed at OL_0 as a whole was responsible for an upward shift of Q curve from $Q(T_1)$ to $Q(T_2)$, and not any segment of OL_0. Thus, once L_0L_1 labour is declared redundant, it will have further adverse impact on size of market, unless the wage rate (and wage bill) for OL_1 labour can compensate for the wage rate (and wage bill) of OL_0 labour employment. The implicit assumption is that wage bill (most of it) understood by the cardinal indicator of consumption propensity goes to be spent in the market (demand).

The implication is that technological improvement-led labour redundancy is labour (knowledge) made, while capital takes advantage of it by non-realization (non-marketing) of higher volume of output produced. Thus, capital-ownership, via market constraint or capital accumulation, declares redundancy of labour. Elimination (exit) of a section of workers cannot solve the problem, because it would accentuate market constraints. It may be difficult to identify that section of workers, who are redundant since all the previously employed workers were responsible for coordinated action in the output space and technological improvement. Whatever we have said so far rests on labour-led technological improvement.

Let us consider a second situation where two products (or, n products, n>2) are produced (and used) in an interdependent way. We assume that there is no prior information to any of the firms producing these products about technological improvement in the other firm(s). As a concrete case, we take the case of firms producing pen (writing), ink (used for pouring inside the pen), and blotting paper (used to soak ink on the writing paper). Technological improvement in the firm that produces pen may lead to ultimate non-use of ink and hence exit of blotting paper. By implication, workers previously engaged in ink and blotting paper manufacturing firms will have to face redundancy or exit. This redundancy is delinked from technological improvement, if any, in the concerned products (ink, blotting paper) where the workers previously were safely employed. Here, the substitution in use of a product (of a variety) A (say, pen) leads to exit of products B (ink) and C (blotting paper). The redundancy in labour could also come in product A (pen) whose end-use pattern is altered by technological change. We considered this in the previous case (Fig. 1). What we stress here is an unforeseen (in absence of prior information) but abruptly declared redundancy of labour by controllers of technology (firm).

Now consider the third situation. Let there be prior information about technological change, within the firm and in the frame of interdependent firms. The labourers come to know at a certain date that they are going to be declared redundant. What do they do?

(IV) Where do workers go when they are declared redundant?

We assume that a worker joins a job, independent of his own choice and often in conditions of ignorance. He has acquired some general skill (knowledge) and some particular skill. This knowledge is primarily linked with how to get a job done, given the freedom (time, materials and machines, favourable environment) to the worker. The alienation of the potential worker (job seeker) from most of the required freedom in a capitalist mode of production always keeps him as a potential victim. The firm-specific potential victimization could be overcome by being mobile across firms. This is, however, conditioned by acquiring multiple skills. In addition, the corporate attachment or community culture within a particular firm, where the concerned workers are initially absorbed may obstruct any mobility of this workforce. From the viewpoint of the particular firm, such an attachment of the workforce is never blamed unless and until the workers are blamed at a mature stage of production. We explained the emergence of this mature stage by technological improvement.

Even if the workers are willing to be mobile, their knowledge of wage and non-wage terms of employment in other jobs is limited. If we assume that the workers are aware of the existence of the wage-differential in similar job for which they seem to be employable, then it makes sense that, *ceteris paribus*, labour mobility will be a direct function of wage-differential. If the labour market is perfectly competitive, then the workers are rational optimizers. In practice, the labour market is heterogeneous and imperfect. In this situation, labour mobility, if any, is wage-intensive and there come non-wage factors and forces to cause immobility of workers.

Underdeveloped economies in general are characterized by immobility of workers. This is because they do not have information about better job opportunities elsewhere, if job opportunities exist at all, or because they are unable to move and offer their job skill. Labour mobility as such is conditioned at the beginning by additional job opportunities, and subsequently conditioned by wage flexibility and wage-differential. With no additional labour absorption in the national economy, there may occur intra-and inter-sectoral reallocation of labour. However, in a state of increasing population, it would imply increasing unemployment. Thus, effective labour mobility also requires increasing job opportunities.

Mixed capitalist economies like India are subject to state control via economic planning. The industrial system has evolved in such a way as to make the establishments 'internally closed'. This allows entry into the establishments at the lowest level or provides limited entry points at the middle and upper levels. Most of the positions in the establishments are filled through internal promotions, offering little opportunities for competition. Thus, there come institutional-cum-administrative barriers to entry and mobility of labourers across both public and private sectors within such mixed economies. As labour mobility requires execution of additional responsibilities (like housing, etc.) by the establishments, it is generally discouraged. In underdeveloped economies in particular, non-contractual, productivity-neutral labour employment based on provision for time-scale salary and seniority-based uplift leads to offer the individual employed in the same firm higher designation and probably higher degradation. This is not to imply that the quality degradation of a worker is a direct function of maturity by age. What we imply here is the workers' reluctance to move from low wage certainty in the existing firm to high wage uncertainty in a different firm. This rigidity in labour market is sector-neutral and plan-neutral. It is essentially rooted in socio-political-institutional-cultural set up of the country.

Often inter-industrial mobility of workers is constrained by imposition of political (in) discipline, for example, in terms of absorption of workers in enterprises. This absorption above some wage category is determined by 'political quota'. The industrial establishments often resemble family-centered business, where not only in tiny, informal and unorganized sector but also in organized industrial plants, there is limited entry for 'outsiders'. Often jobs in the high wage occupations or responsible positions are reserved for persons in, or connected with, the affluent society. The country in question may have colonial heritage, where people educated abroad are preferred to those educated inside the country. The job pattern in the existing establishments may be non-innovative or stereotyped where internal workforce is preferred to external ones. Often the nature of entry into the job market is time-tied, making mobility of the workforce non-operational for the stipulated period. Many of such situations are beyond the control of the workforce, either in seeking jobs or in changing jobs.

In addition to above, industrialization brings with it a movement from lower-order technology to higher-order technology. On this trajectory, technology of the workforce may become prone to self-destruction. This is self-destruction because, as we argued in the beginning, only a section of the advanced learners in jobs brought about this trajectory. During the 1990s in the Indian industrial sector, as high as 30 per cent redundancy was estimated in the organized sector which employed around 28 million workers. The 243 operating central public enterprises alone shed 2,00,000 jobs during 1991-97 through means, other than retrenchment. In addition, as high as 15,534 workers were retrenched in organized industrial sector during 1992-97. The Steel Authority of India in the public sector reduced its work force from 2,30,000 in 1996 to 1,80,000 in 1997. In Indian Railways, it has already been estimated that as high as 33 per cent of the workforce is redundant. The Tata Iron and Steel Co. in the private sector have planned recently to downsize its workforce to one-third of its present size (Venkata Ratnam, 1998, pp. 276-377). Across countries in the world economy, as many traditional production functions are displaced by machines, there has been a fall in employment of production workers. This has been accompanied by a redefining of much production work, as the introduction of new technology and new forms of work organization (which tend to complement Information Technology) requires production workers to be more skilled and knowledgeable (ILO, 1999, p. 39). Because of pervasive IT effects in industries and workplace, the newly unskilled workers are declared redundant. There is job destruction along with job creation. The Broken Proprietary Company Limited (BHP) as the largest steel producer in Australia shed its workforce from 9406 in 1990 to 7036 in 1996. The victims were the unskilled iron workers. The reduction in size of the workforce came along with 'up-skilling' and career path development for iron workers who used to acquire skills traditionally (mainly developed on-the-job) without formal training (ILO, 1999, p. 40).

The general downsizing of the workforce thus may rest on the following factors:

(i) Changed product mix and the rapid disappearance of the requirement for traditional skills;

(ii) Changing location of production and obstructed mobility of workers;

(iii) Non-renewal of previously acquired specialization by workers;

(iv) Abrupt effort by the owners of non-labour resources to accommodate the entry of transnational capital in the firm;

(v) Managerial inefficiency in diversification of products to compensate the probable contraction in market faced by the firm;

(vi) Managerial apathy towards R&D and training for skill formation of workers;

(vii) Application of capital-deepening technical progress;

(viii) Downsizing of less efficient workers on the basis of intra-firm efficiency parameters accepted by the owners of non-labour resources.

At the operational level, the downsizing of workers declared redundant occurs by withdrawal of state support to loss-making public sector enterprises (PSEs), closure of industrial units (both in public and private) declared sick, privatization of PSEs and hence adoption of hire and fire methods by managers in private enterprises (Chandra, 1999, p. 32; Alam and Mishra, 1998, p. 279). There comes downsizing of the workforce not because of absolute inter-temporal reducing productivity per worker. The scope for downsizing may crop up from relative productivity. The changes in technology and work organization, often complementing each other, have resulted in a shift in the nature of skill demand. The changing character of new technologies requires workers who can learn and adapt to these changes quickly and efficiently. Though the skill itself may not be "higher", the ability to master it quickly and use it productively calls for a high level of confidence and familiarity that favours the higher skilled (ILO, 1999, p. 46). The relative obsolescence and degradation of a section of the workforce is manifested when there emerge a relatively advanced section of the manpower within the firm or even outside. The relatively advanced section is responsible for inventions and innovations. Employment of this advanced section in a fully operated (optimal capacity) firm will have a tendency to crowd out the section declared redundant.

There has to be a method to offer the workers, an avenue, to go once redundancy is identified. One such avenue being practiced in Indian industries is offering Voluntary Retirement Scheme (VRS) to the workers. In its attempt to realize maximum (output) benefits from 'learning effect' the enterprises may plan rationalization of its workforce by offering VRS. The difficulty in execution of such a scheme is that the more efficient (by learning) workers at the middle age (median age by service span generally understood) may opt for such VRS, while the less efficient workers stay. This is because for the former it works as a money supporting force for vertical (or at least horizontal) mobility, while for the latter safety remains by non-opting for VRS. This is likely to have reflections on the quality of the product, state of technology and work environment inside the plant that opted for and executed VRS (Rameshan, 1998, p. 107). The general framework that we conceived at the beginning remains undisturbed, namely, workforce-led technological improvement and technology-led exit of workforce. This technology-determined exit of a section of the workforce has to be rehabilitated to socially useful old technology-based jobs. This is, however, constrained by the efforts of the people without economic jobs for entry.

(V) What is to be done for rehabilitation?

The question on rehabilitation is an economic question in addition to being an ethical as well as a social question. It is an ethical question because the initial competence of a worker for inclusion in a plant cannot at ease wither away, because of inter-temporal relative (inter-personal) less competence. It is a social question because the service rendered so far by the workers inside a plant was very much based on social cooperation. In other words, attainment of the initial PPC was very much a reflection of cooperation among workers at all layers inside the plant. The question is economic, because the size of market is contracted by the long-term displacement of workers. The implicit assumption is that, the wage base of the residue workers cannot compensate for the wage bill now being truncated because of labour displacement. The issue is not a hypothetical conflict between new employment of more efficient workers (from the viewpoint of technology and capital), but is a question of assuring the initially employed workers, a notion of safety by wage-income and work opportunity inside the plant. There is no reason to delink wage-income from work-productivity. Rehabilitation of a section of the currently employed workforce is a relevant question if the section can be identified. To counter obsolescence and to ensure rehabilitation, the following measures are suggested:

(i) Ensuring both general and particular skill at the level of the plant as soon as the individual is absorbed;

(ii) Implementing job rotation programmes inside a plant;

(iii) Ensuring continuous training for the workforce inside plants to offset both deterioration and obsolescence;

(iv) Counseling for workers to understood their perceptions about the job, their attitude to work etc;

(v) Ensuring not only on-the-job training, but also on-the-job competency test based on training;

(vi) Making people inside the plant understand the complementarity between machine and man;

(vii) Developing responsible trade unionism for understanding the initial labour displacing effect of the machine;

(viii) Ensuring on-site and off-site training, particularly for those workers who face exit by rationalization of the plant in response to high-tech industrialization;

(ix) Income-support for conducting training programmes for workers;

(x) Developing or adopting diversified products by the advanced section of the workforce so that the existing workforce can be reallocated;

(xi) Promoting sunrise industries in case some products belong to sunset enterprises.

Training is a major exercise to keep workers on-the-job where they were employed years ago (ILO, 1999, p. 187). There is, however, no alternative to generating the scope for labour employment by selection of appropriate products and technologies. There is enough scope for labour-based and local resource-based technologies that offer increasing scope for employment generation. The examples may include both productive physical infrastructure and social infrastructure. The first category includes land reclamation, minor dams, irrigation system, drainage, link roads, canals, etc., while the second one includes schools at multi levels and health centers (ILO, 2000, p. 163). Rehabilitation of workers declared redundant thus, is not only a function of training of workers, but is also a function of selection of labour absorbing products/plants/sectors. Market alone may sometimes show wrong signals, particularly when the rehabilitation question of the handicapped workers (by birth or on-the-job) is considered. There may arise the need for providing employment subsidy.

(VI) Concluding Comments

Resistance to technological changes will be much less if the workers have the confidence in the ability of the entrepreneurs, including the government, to provide alternative jobs. To be brief, the workers join jobs independent of their own will. The technology applied is not within the jurisdiction of the workers, though present machines are the products of the past workers engaged in the same or in a different plant. But the present use of that machine is not within the discretion of the workers engaged at present nor could the past workers deny production of the machines produced in the past and used at present. The capital that goes to buy or hire machine and labour hour is independent of the choice of the workers. The obsolescence of a section of the workers is dependent on introduction of new technology and hence time-dependent. The inherent inequality in brainpower must bring about this technology-led redundancy of a section of the workforce. By absolute productivity, this section may justify their wage rate being received. The inter-temporal productivity of this section declared redundant might have also increased to justify enhanced wage rate. Nevertheless, this section declared redundant could not escape relative deterioration in terms of productivity, that is, relative to the more advanced sections. A section of the workforce at best can try to delay the process of their own obsolescence but cannot stop it. This section of the workforce becomes more vulnerable if they were in plants that are now in sunset category. A plant becomes a sunset plant at a stage of production because of factors beyond the control of the workers employed at present. The factors that determine whether a plant will be in the sunset category will depend on ownership and control of capital, technology and rationalization of the plant. If the plant is rationalized by which we mean downsizing manpower, then the section that pays is the displaced workers. The assumption is that the rationalization is labour-saving. There is the threat that if the firm does not initiate rationalization, there emerge the problems of the exit of the plant itself. The task is to establish sunrise plants, plan localization of plants appropriate for existing skill of the displaced workforce, ensuring new employment of the workers displaced from sunset plants and plants set for rationalization. The tasks rest on the workers at multi-layers in a plant (acquiring skill, by job rotation, for example), the managers in a plant (by diversification of products and technological choice) and the extra-plant authority (for example, the institutions and the state by actions and policies).

References

Alam, Moneer and S. N. Mishra (1998), "Structural Reforms and Employment Issues in India: A Case of Industrial Labour", *The Indian Journal of Labour Economics*, Vol. 41, No. 2.

Chandra, Ashoka (1999), "Retraining for Redeployment: NRF Initiative and Challenge in Training", *The Indian Journal of Labour Economics*, Vol. 42, No. 1.

Hicks, J. R. (1971), *The Social Framework*, Oxford University Press, London.

ILO (1999), *World Employment Report*, International Labour Office, Bookwell, Delhi.

Venkata Ratnam, C. S. (1998), "Economic Reforms and Labour", *Productivity*, Vol. 39, No. 3.

9

Technology and Economic Development of a Developing Economy: A Theoretical Note

The concern for commodity production and economic development is as old as the birth of economics as a branch of scientific analysis (Chakravorty, 1988; Kuznets, 1961, p. 13; Kuznets, 1965, pp. 63, 83-84, 105; Kerr, 1993, pp. 5, 9). It is well established by now that the positive volume of physical output and positive rate of growth of output within a national economy may fail to ensure the objectives of removing poverty and attaining self-reliance. Thus, a fresh look is necessary on the question of technology that converts commodities into commodities and to examine not only the technical feasibility of economic growth but also to examine if that growth can be ensured by the people who are the cause and consequence of growth, and hence also to examine the nature of that growth.

In our analytical frame we assume that (i) production of commodities is a reflection of social cooperation, (ii) a process of growth visible to all has to be shared by all, and (iii) the state has to ensure macro-economic growth and balances.

Section I of the paper offers a brief note on the interplay of market, state and technology. Section II visualizes a scheme on product-cum-technology association for formation of market to ensure development of a late-starter. Finally, in section III we chalk out the implications of the scheme.

(I) Market, State and Technology

The commodity-technology association for the economy may be written as:

$$\{Q,T\} \equiv \{Q_i,T_j\} \qquad (1)$$

Where Q is the vector of producible commodities and T is a vector of technologies in production of Q.

$$Q \equiv \{Q_i\}, i = 1,2,...,n$$
$$T \equiv \{T_j\}, j = 1,2,...,m \qquad (2)$$

Where $m \geq n$, on the assumption of non-identical technology for any two commodities. T denotes the nature of association between human (labour) and non-human resources. While the conventional production function explains the movement of Q along a single product curve, T is an operator that explains the shift of the curve. T covers certain characteristics like scale of operations, nature of products, etc. (Stewart, 1977, p. 2). Q and T are determined not independently but together.

Let the commodities be Q_1, Q_2, ..., Q_n decided to be produced by n individuals A_1, A_2, ..., A_n, with associated technologies T_1, T_2, ..., T_n. Here T_1 is one specific way of converting natural resources by A_1 to produce Q_1 (consumable and tradeable). T_1 is the best available technology among alternative technologies and by application becomes best practiced technology for Q_1. Similar is for T_2, ..., T_n.

With respect to technological change the production system alters its character from a simple interdependence to a complex interdependence. Some producers outcompete others when they accumulate capital (machinery, tools, etc.) given the initial equivalence in exchange of commodities unchanged and convert others into potential sellers of labour power. Here comes the questions of adoption and acceptability of the altered situation, the power of the society to absorb shocks following the advent of new technology, and hence the necessity of consensus among economic agents (actual and potential), the formation of the rules of the game (in using technologies, producing output, etc.,) and need for the supervision by a competent referee (market and/or state).

We consider the state, in a society passing through capitalist transition, as a decision-making authority trying in principle, to ensure mutuality of interests of antagonistic social groups and individuals (Kurien, 1987, p. AN-26; Bardhan, 1984, pp. 32-39; Patnaik, 1984, pp. 1251-1260; Alavi, 1982, pp. 289-307). State is the visible hand which directs the course of development. We stress on formation of market which is dependent on growth of money-based exchange in final commodities, growth of employment based on wage labour, and a developed money (credit) market. State is the institution which recognizes and rationalizes production relation as a particular social relation in a capitalist society based on the rules of exclusion of paupers, or what we call state recognition of market power. But then for the market to survive, expand and ensure macro-economic growth, again the state has to step in. If market power is recognized and accepted in principle by the state by guaranteeing security of private property, then accumulation by the powerful, keeping the corollary in mind, is conditional upon state action viz., expansion of market or inclusion of more people in production and exchange. This may, however, invite new contradictions, unless this inclusion principle is backed by polity and people inside jobs, because the process of capitalist industrialization is by nature based on the principle of exclusion and exit.

The paradox is not that the advantages of growth, viz., accumulation, increasingly accrue to those who control material resources. The paradox lies in the existence of a very small actual market based on wage-labour relative to a big potential market, in a situation when the rewards of inflation go to the capitalists. This is the context where the task of market formation and expansion for development cannot be considered in isolation from the state.

To be brief, the formation and functioning of market is conditional upon recognition of private property by the state. Ownership of marketable property implies market power, which is by initial condition skewed. Thus, unless there is a policy-determined distribution of economic power of individuals, or redistribution of market power, the market will continue to malfunction. This necessitates state action. We explore this in section II.

(II) Product-Cum-Technology Association and Formation of Market

The scheme we are going to construct, includes the following variables in real terms:

Q = National Output
Q_A = Output in the rural economy centering agriculture
Q_1 = Output in the urban economy centering industry
Q_F = Agricultural (Rural) consumer goods output
Q_{NF} = Non-consumable agricultural (rural) output
Q_C = Non-agricultural consumer goods output (Urban/ Industrial)
Q_k = Capital (Investment) goods output (Urban/Industrial)
Y = National Income
C = National Consumption
I = National Investment
L = Total Labour available in the economy (Population in the working age)
L_A = Labour Employment (Rural/Agricultural)
L_I = Labour Employment (Urban/Industrial)

The equations are the following

$$Q = Q_A + Q_I \quad (1)$$
$$Q_A = Q_F + Q_{NF} \quad (2)$$

$$Q_1 = Q_C + Q_K \quad (3)$$
$$Y = C + I \quad (4)$$
$$C = Q_F + Q_C \quad (5)$$
$$I = Q_{NF} + Q_K \quad (6)$$
$$Y = Q \quad (7)$$
$$L = L_A + L_I \quad (8)$$

Form either (4), (5) and (6), or, from (1), (2), (3) and (7)

$$Y = Q_F + Q_C + Q_K + Q_{NF} \quad (9)$$

Equation (9) shows an output-composition of effective demand (Keynesian-type) where the frame is taken to be autarkic. However, intervention by government/trade can be accommodated to keep our frame undisturbed. Let us look at the Leontief-type input-output frame (Table 1).

Considering only final demand, we have

$$Q_F \geq Q_{FA} + Q_{FI} \quad (10)$$

$$Q_C \geq Q_{CA} + Q_{CI} \quad (11)$$

Equations (10) and (11) show supply-demand balance for consumer goods (agricultural and non-agricultural).

Thus, derived from equations (5), (10) and (11), decomposition of consumption demand may be seen from equation (12):

$$C \geq Q_{FA} + Q_{CA} + Q_{FI} + Q_{CI} \quad (12)$$

where

$Q_{FA} + Q_{CA}$ = Rural Consumption Demand
$Q_{FI} + Q_{CI}$ = Urban Consumption Demand

Similarly, from Equation (6) and Table 1, decomposition of investment demand may be seen from Equation (13):

Table 1

Input-Output Frame

Commodities To / *Commodities From*			*Final Demand*			*Total Output*
	Rural	*Urban*	*Rural*	*Urban*	*Government Purchase and/or Export*	
Rural	Q_{NF1}	Q_{NF2}	Q_{FA}	Q_{FI}	Q_{FG} and/or Q_{FX}	Q_A
Urban	Q_{K1}	Q_{K2}	Q_{CA}	Q_{CI}	Q_{IG} and/or Q_{IX}	Q_I
Labour	L_A	L_I				L

$$I = Q_{NF1} + Q_{K1} + Q_{NF2} + Q_{K2} \quad (13)$$

Where
$Q_{NF1} + Q_{K1}$ = Rural (Input) Investment Demand
$Q_{NF2} + Q_{K2}$ = Urban (Input) Investment Demand

Obviously from Equations (4), (12) and (13), we get

$$Y \geq Q_{FA} + Q_{CA} + Q_{FI} + Q_{CI} + Q_{NF1} + Q_{K1} + Q_{NF2} + Q_{K2} \quad (14)$$

Considering alternative uses of output, we have, from Table 1,

$$Q_A \geq Q_{NF1} + Q_{NF2} + Q_{FA} + Q_{FI} \quad (15)$$

$$Q_I \geq Q_{K1} + Q_{K2} + Q_{CA} + Q_{CI} \quad (16)$$

Equations (15) and (16) show supply demand balance equations for agricultural and industrial goods. Equations (10), (11), (12), (14), (15), (16) are balanced by entry of government/trade.

The production functions in this system are:

$$Q_A = Q_A(Q_{NF1}, Q_{K1}, L_A) \quad (17)$$

$$Q_I = Q_I(Q_{NF2}, Q_{K2}, L_1) \quad (18)$$

The initial distribution of power (ownership over resources and hence revealed market power) determines the initial product and associated technology. The technology-in-use, in turn, specifies the nature of commodity and market (demand).

Implicit in (17) and (18) are the following observations:

(i) Q_{NF1} and Q_{NF2} have been produced by L_A at a previous period; similarly Q_{K1} and Q_{K2} produced by L_I at a previous period.

(ii) L_A is producing Q_{NF1} and Q_{NF2} as components of Q_A, which in turn feeds L_I, L_I in turn produces Q_{K1} and Q_{K2} as components of Q_I. Thus Q_A is the basic commodity and L_A is its basic source for production.

(iii) L_I comes in the economy in its urban part at a developed (industrial) stage of production when surplus of Q_A is ready to be released to feed L_I.

Let us write equations (17) and (18) as the following:

$$Q_A = Q_A(T_A) \tag{19}$$

$$Q_I = Q_I(T_1) \tag{20}$$

Where T_A denotes technology related to rural output and T_I denotes technology related to urban output, where technologies are thought to be separate sectorally/spatially, which in practice are not.

Equations (19) and (20) actually exhibit a nature of association and not a one-way causation. Considering rural economy, e.g., T_A itself incorporates one specific type of, and its changing, output-mix. T_A is dynamic (historically evolved via learning by doing) in the sense that at a particular point of time the best practiced process is adopted allowing for a better (budding) process at a later date, where by process we mean the way of combining invisible and visible inputs, 'best practiced' in the sense of having power to generate output by least possible time and allowing increasing labour absorption (via creation of more working hours). Similar is for T_I.

Actually Q_A and Q_I are output vectors:

$Q_A = (Q_{Ai})$, i = 1,2,....,n; n denotes a set of agricultural products.

$Q_I = (Q_{Ij})$, j = 1,2,....,m; m denotes a set of industrial products.

Similarly, T_A and T_I are technology vectors:

$T_A = (T_{Ai})$

$T_I = (T_{Ij})$

There is no *a priori* technology ordering. Selection of technology is very much product-specific.

We may write (17) and (18), from the demand side, as

$$Q_A = F(M_A) \tag{21}$$

$$Q_I = F(M_I) \tag{22}$$

Where M_A denotes market (demand) for Q_A, M_I denotes market (demand) for Q_I

Equations (21) and (22) show an association between demand and output and not a one-way causation. Adding foreign market does not alter our analytical frame.

Alternatively, by market we could have meant (i) Rural market for Q_A and Q_I, (ii) Urban market for Q_A and Q_I. The question is how is this market (M_A + M_I) formed and how does it function.

Let us look at the product-technology association to get an answer.

If the urban economy is satisfied with the supply of industrial consumer goods and capital goods (i.e., if intra-urban commodity flows are fixed at a predetermined level), i.e.,

$$Q_{K2} = \overline{Q}_{K2} > 0 and Q_{C1} = \overline{Q}_{C1} > 0 \tag{23}$$

then the problem is to ensure industrial growth via raising the output of industrial consumer goods (Q_{CA}) and capital goods (Q_{KI}). These goods are to be sold to the rural economy. If the state does not rely on relief (welfare approach) measures (which it cannot afford to for long) or on ad hocism reflected in target-group-oriented programme (which necessarily fails), it has to rely on growth approach, in our context, via raising Q_A.

If the urban economy does not purchase any additional Q_A, i.e., if rural output necessary for urban people is ensured (via public distribution system or otherwise), i.e., if

$$Q_{NF2} = \overline{Q}_{NF2} and Q_{F1} = \overline{Q}_{F1} \tag{24}$$

then the process of output-income generation in rural economy is impeded (in absence of increasing income flowing to rural economy from urban economy).

Then intra-rural economy production and exchange work via Q_{NF1} and Q_{FA}.

Whether or not the total or truncated rural-urban flows work, we may get product-cum-technology association (in operation or planned) to be reflected in formation of rural market for (urban) industrial goods.

Let w denote wage rate and W, wage share. This wage share can work as proxy for rural income and wage rate as per capita rural income. Then the choice of product-specific selection of technology leads to determination of wage-labour employment, in turn, formation of rural market.

$$\begin{aligned}
Q_{A1}(T_{Ai}) &= (L_{A_{1i}}, \omega_{A_{1i}}) = (\omega_{A_{1i}}) = (M_{A_{1i}}) \\
Q_{A2}(T_{Ai}) &= (L_{A_{2i}}, \omega_{A_{2i}}) = (\omega_{A_{2i}}) = (M_{A_{2i}}) \\
&\cdots\cdots\cdots\cdots\cdots\cdots\cdots\cdots \\
Q_{AN}(T_{Ai}) &= (L_{A_{ni}}, \omega_{A_{ni}}) = (\omega_{A_{ni}}) = (M_{A_{ni}})
\end{aligned} \tag{25}$$

Once the rural market is formed (expanded) via product embodied selection of technologies, it stimulates demand for Q_1 (i.e., Q_{CA} and Q_{K1}). The size of rural market for industrial goods corresponds to the pattern of wage-employment via the product-cum-technology specification. If this specification changes, size of rural market also will change (and vice versa) to alter the demand for industrial goods and industrial growth.

Given (23) and (24), we get from (14),

$$Y \geq (Q_{FA} + Q_{NF1}) + (Q_{CA} + Q_{K1}) + F, \quad (14a)$$

$$Where\ F = Q_{NF2} + Q_{K2} + Q_{CI} + Q_{FI} > 0 \text{ and fixed}$$

Thus, following our scheme, an effect on Y (or Q) over time is felt via rising (Q_{FA} + Q_{NF1}), associated with rising (Q_{K1} + Q_{CA}).

Now from (15), taking equality,

$$Q_A = (Q_{NF1} + Q_{FA}) + (Q_{NF2} + Q_{F1}) + (Q_{FG} + Q_{FX}) \quad (15a)$$

$$or, Q_A = \alpha Q_A + K + A \quad (26)$$

where α is the proportion of Q_A used within rural economy (as inputs and final consumption demand).

$$By(24), K = \overline{Q}_{NF2} + \overline{Q}_{F1} > 0$$

Here A = Q_{FG} + Q_{FX}, where A may be treated as an autonomous variable by government (policy) intervention.

Taking total differential of (26)

$$dQ_A = \alpha dQ_A dK + dA \quad (27)$$

If dK = 0 by differential of (24), dA has to be positive for positive dQ_A with implications derived from government intervention and/or trade.

If, however, (24) is relaxed in favour of dK>0, then

$$\frac{dQ_A}{dK} = \frac{1}{1-\alpha} > 1 \text{ with dA} = 0 \quad (28)$$

And

$$\frac{dQ_A}{dZ} = \frac{1}{1-\alpha} \text{ where Z} = \text{K} + \text{A, dA} > 0 \quad (29)$$

In (26), $Q_{NF1} + Q_{FA} = \alpha Q_A$, $0 < á < 1$

As $\alpha \rightarrow 1$, $(Q_{NF1} + Q_{FA}) \rightarrow Q_A$;

And $(K + A) \rightarrow 0$

Or $Z \rightarrow 0$

and hence, equation (26) does not yield any solution.

The implication is, for an effective functioning of the system, α will have to be less than unity. The lower the value of α over time, the more the strength of the system for release of Q_A or the higher is the marketable (and marketed through appropriate policy decision by government) agricultural surplus for urban labourers plus government purchase plus trade. The route signals development.

Let (26) be rewritten as

$$Q_A = \alpha_1 Q_A + \alpha_2 Q_A + Z \quad (26a)$$

α_1 and α_2 being the percentages of Q_A used as inputs and finally consumed respectively by the rural people, i.e.,

$$Q_{NF1} = \alpha_1 Q_A, 0 < \alpha_1, \alpha_2 < 1$$

$$Q_{FA} = \alpha_2 Q_A, (\alpha_1 + \alpha_2) < 1$$

Thus, taking total differential of (26a) we get

$$\frac{dQ_A}{dZ} = \frac{1}{1-(\alpha_1 + \alpha_2)} \quad (30)$$

Possibilities from (30):

(i) If $(\alpha_1 + \alpha_2) \longrightarrow 1$, we get our earlier conclusion just as

$\alpha \longrightarrow 1$

(ii) if $\alpha_2 \longrightarrow 1$ (initially it may happen in a primitive subsistence agriculture in an LDC with no government intervention).

Then $(\alpha_1 Q_A + Z) \longrightarrow 0$

And separately α_1, Q_A and Z, each tends to zero, if they are not offsetting but reinforcing with respect to their effect on Q_A.

For Q_A ‘‘‘ 0

logically $\alpha_1 \longrightarrow 0$

If thus the whole of Q_A is consumed by the rural people, industrial growth becomes food import-dependent, government cannot allow this policy for long.

(iii) If $\alpha_1 \longrightarrow 0$ (only via strict government control or application of force), then as before $\alpha_2 \longrightarrow 0$.

This implies famine in rural economy/migration/import of food by government, etc. In any case, it reveals policy failure or self-defeating policy of the government.

Thus, subject to the constraints imposed by (23) and (24) (i.e., urban constraints), a mechanism of $Q_A - T_A - M_A$ association gets reflected in raising $(Q_{NF1} + Q_{FA})$, operator being the parameter α(or, $\alpha_1 + \alpha_2$).

Increasing rural output gets reflected in increasing demand for industrial goods.

Let us look at the equation (14a) then,

$$Y \geq (Q_{FA} + Q_{NF1}) + (Q_{K1} + Q_{CA}) + F,$$

Where F = Urban Demand (for consumption and investment)>0

If we relax the constancy constraint i.e. if F>0 and not fixed,

then

$$\frac{\dot{F}}{F} >< 0 \Rightarrow \text{better/worse growth prospect.}$$

While: $\frac{\dot{F}}{F} > 0$ is a welcome preposition.

$\frac{\dot{F}}{F} < 0$ is to be encountered by internal export

(government purchase and/or external export (via policy decision by government).

(III) Implications of the Scheme

Our scheme aims at output-employment oriented home-market-dependent development. Since economic development is an upward movement in the structure of commodity production, and since command differential as a derivation from application of initial technology by individuals leads to a new set of commodities (and technologies), so the question regarding the possibility of economic development as a historical process of participation of man in commodity production is relevant.

Commodity is the wheel that makes man move: movement from the point of production to the point of consumption. The system develops as follows:

Initial technology ⟶ Initial output ⟶ Learning by doing ⟶ Knowledge ⟶ Improved technology ⟶ Expansion in production boundary ⟶ Development.

Commodity production of a particular nature (technology associated) leads to the development of a specific relation between participants, between participants and non-participants, between both on the one hand, and nature on the other. This is the point which warrants state action as a shock absorber. Assuming that the state is strongly committed in principle to generate rural market for industrial goods (as the size of home market is basically related to existence of market in rural regions in developing economies), we chalk out our scheme.

The choice of products and technologies by rural people aims at reducing working hours per labourer as well as raising wage per hour. Planning by the state in this context has to explore the possibilities of raising labour productivity that may help release a section of labourers from dependence on land. These released labourers may be absorbed in rural infrastructure and related public works, thus maximizing the participation rate (the ratio of number of labourers employed to what is available). This, in turn, is expected to generate market.

The strategy of development based on rural industrialization in the early phase may fail to generate rural demand for higher order industrial goods, given the absolute extent of poverty and poor infrastructure in rural regions of such economies. But, if industrial production is to have a rural market for its viability, initial product-technology ordering in rural economy has to be need-based and socially oriented. After the basic consumption necessities are met, the increasing income will chase industrial goods in an ascending order (World Bank, 1978, p. 30; ILO, 1974, p. 511; Griffin and Khan, 1978, pp. 299-300).

Our scheme aims at checking an initial leakage of purchasing power from the rural economy. For this, planning has to ensure the rural inhabitants' absorption in non-farm rural activities and create conditions for feedback of investible resources in rural economy in particular, and for removal of infrastructural constraints in general, operating in the rural regions of these economies and in the same process maximize individual and collective income and commodity entitlements (UN 1978, p. 55). Since production and generation of income move together in order, if output-mix-cum-technology decisions are taken by the lower strata of population through e.g., decentralized planning, inflation of any type is supposed not to neutralize the commodity entitlement of the participating agents (Streeten and Burki, 1978, p. 414).

We rely on development and use of rural need-based technology primarily because technology is useful to convert community-and-caste-based isolation into a production-based interdependence. We stress on rural resource-specific technology secondarily because the endemic nature of mass poverty and inequality is derived not only from differences in initial private ownership over resources but also how the resources are organized and used in production (Cahan, 1994-95, p. 405). Success of planning for independent development along this path depends on a strong state commitment to initiate the activities, which in turn, depends on a strong state commitment to initiate the activities, which in turn, depends on conscious participation of people in decision-making processes and centres.

References

Alavi, Hamza (1982), "State and Class under peripheral Capitalism", in Alavi, H. and T. Shanin, (eds), *Introduction to the Sociology of Developing Socieities*, Macmillan.

Bardhan, P. (1984), *The Political Economy of Development in India*, Oxford University Press, Delhi.

Cahan, Jean Axelrad, (1994-95), "The Concept of Property in Marx's Theory of History: A Defence of the Autonomy of the Socio-economic Base", *Science and Society*, Vol. 58, No. 4, Winter.

Chakrovorty, Skhamoy (1988), "Development of Development Thinking", *Arthavijnan*, Vol. XXX, No. 2, June.

Griffin, K. and A. R. Khan (1978), "Poverty in the third World: Ugly Facts and Fancy Models", *World Development*, Vol. 6, No. 3.

International Labour Organization (ILO) (1974), "Sharing in Development: A Programme of Employment, Equity and Growth for the Philippines", ILO Geneva.

Kerr, Prue (1993), "Adam Smith's Theory of Growth and Technological Change Re-visited", *Contributions to Political Economy*, Vol. 12.

Kurien, C. T. (1987), "State and Market in Economic Process: Some Basic Issues", *Economic and Political Weekly*, Vol. XXII, Annual Number, May.

Kuznets, Simon (1961), *Six Lectures on Economic Growth*, The Free Press, USA.

——————— (1965), *Economic Growth and Structure*, W. W. Norton and Co., New York.

Patnaik, P. (1984), "Market Question and Capitalist Development in India", *Economic and Political Weekly*, Vol. XIX, Annual Number, August.

Stewart, F. (1977), *Technology and Underdevelopment*, Macmillan.

Streetem, P. and S. J. Burki (1978), "Basic Needs: Some Issues", *World Development*, Vol. 6, No. 3.

United Nations (1978), "The Significance of Rural Housing in Integrated Rural Development", Department of Economic and Social Affairs, New York.

World Bank (1978), "Rural Enterprise and Non-farm Employment", A World Bank Paper, January.

10

Influx of Forced Labour: Nature and Causes

An individual becomes a worker by doing any work independent of the time rule (labour hour) and collects/produces products for herself (including her family). The worker always exists as a social category, while labour exists as an economic category. Capitalism converts a worker into a labourer willing to sell labour power (a commodity) to the buyer (another individual or owner/controller of non-labour resources) at the prevailing (or agreed upon) price (wage rate). Labour (hour) becomes the root or cause of all products, that is the time expression of labour power embedded in the labourer (Harris - White, 2004, p. 17). The labour hour gets concrete shape in products and services. Institutions convert a social category into an economic category, and hence a 'worker' becomes a 'labourer'. An individual joins a job, the first one, independent of his own will, and dependent on prevailing laws, customs, practices etc. as shown by institutions. In a gross sense, thus, any 'labour' is 'forced'. We, however, study here the case where the very joining a job in involuntary, in the sense that it happens in a condition of helplessness. The job becomes 'forced' in nature if the workers like to leave it in presence of 'any alternative job' and/or if one does not feel comfortable in the current job. A job may also show self-exploitation and hence 'forced' in nature. 'Forced' labour is mainly an urban phenomenon, when the worker feels compelled (forced) to leave the root (village and land-linked activities), at least, temporarily to migrate to urban region in search of 'any' job for support income.

We present in this paper the nature and causes of the influx of workers to the cities in search of any paid work. We refer to the nature of forced labour or self-exploitation as it happens in case of rickshaw pulling in urban job market. The study centers on the city of Allahabad.

The rest of the paper is structured as follows. In Section I, we briefly present the nature of urbanization in terms of influx and exodus of population as potential workers. In Section II we look into the nature of forced labour as seen in case of rickshaw pulling over time in the city of Allahabad. In Section III we look into the landholding pattern of the rickshaw pullers in their root, that is, where they migrate from, and occupational pattern and income of the households of rickshaw pullers. In Section IV we analyze the reasons for the migration of the rickshaw pullers. In Section V we raise the question if a job like rickshaw pulling is forced in nature or if it is self-exploitation. Finally, in Section VI we offer some suggestions.

(I) Urbanization: Influx and Exodus

Urbanization is a process of agglomeration of population that get settled within a narrow boundary relative to the size of settled population showing high density of population per square kilometer. Natural increase in population or shift of existing urban boundary or reclassification of areas leads to formation of towns/ cities. Composition of the towns/cities shows urban regions.

The offshoot of urbanization gets reflected in net migration of population in a frame of rural-urban inflows and outflows of population, setting up of industries in urban boundaries, increasing percentage of population waiting at the gates of the industries, deruralization, and formation of both formal and informal labour market with increasing reserve army of labourers. The consequences may be proletarianization, pauperization, slumization, and criminalization. There is no escape from urbanization even if it leads to the consequences seen as 'bad' for humanity.

In conventional literature urbanization is measured by certain parameters like density of population, percentage of population engaged in secondary and tertiary occupations, production of land-delinked goods, improved infrastructure, easy communication etc. Urban-Rural differential will be manifest in terms of all these parameters, like urban region showing much higher population density, much higher percentage of population in secondary and tertiary services, increasing shift from nature (land, climate) dependent production, increasing processing of goods, and use of higher- order technology. There are offshoots of these indicators linked with urbanization.

A particular location may be attractive to some individuals to use the location economically and hence attract population for ultimate settlement. These locations may be resource rich, linked by railways, or by ports etc. A corollary is development of the location as industrial growth centre and generating scope for employment in the centre and in the periphery. Movement of people from outside is a corollary. The probability of getting jobs, wage-differential and hence higher standard of living, better education and health act as a 'pitcher plant' in the urban economy (Majumder, 2004). A city is a constituent of this urban economy.

The carrying capacity and vibrancy of a city is understood by the size of the settled population in a city, the quality of the people in terms of understanding the scope and nature of work, and the actual frequency of people moving in and moving out. This, at the same time, shows mobility of workers in search of economic occupations. That a city is economically attractive is partially proved by the influx while the exodus shows the search for outside jobs by some of the settled people. For a city that can attract people from outside, it will be prima facie difficult to understand why people move out. One reason could be wage-differential, while there may also be non-economic parameters like heredity-cum-caste determined jobs, prevalence of caste division of labour etc. Potential workers settled inside the city may be reluctant to be engaged in a particular type of job because of cultural taboo.

The influx of people from outside the city covers short-distance influx as well as long-distance influx. The short-distance influx is generally characterized by 'easy come easy go' like entering into the city in the morning and going back at the end of the same day or at the end of the week. The long-distance influx is 'long-stay' type with going home after money/saving is accumulated. The circulation of labour by periodic migration has been recorded in the context of south Gujarat elsewhere (Breman, 1996).

Table 1 India: Urbanization by Settlement of Population, 1901-2001

Year	*Urban Population (Million)*	*Urban Population as Percentage of Total Population*
1901	29.9	10.8
1911	25.9	10.3
1921	28.1	11.2
1931	33.5	12.0
1941	44.2	13.9
1951	62.4	17.3
1961	78.9	18.0
1971	109.1	19.9
1981	159.5	23.3
1991	217.6	25.7
2001	306.9	30.5

Source: Census of India, 2001.

Because of push and pull factors, the population gets settled in urban region. Though in a primarily land (agriculture) dependent economy people would prefer to remain locally confined, economic compulsions often make them unsettled. This unsettlement leads to migration of many types including 'forced' one. Urbanization is a consequence of both voluntary and forced migration of settled population from earlier settled village economy. For the economy of India the trend of urbanization by population is shown in Table 1.

During the twentieth century, over hundred years, urban population as percentage of India's total settled population increased from 10.0 per cent to 30.0 per cent, that is, increased thrice by percentage indicator. For the world as a whole, the percentage of urban population stood at 47.0 in 2001. For the developed countries the percentage stood between 75.0 and 80.0 (Majumder 2004 a). For the most populous state in India that is Uttar Pradesh, the percentage of population settled in urban region stood at around 20.0 per cent during the last one decade (Table 2).

Table 2 Urban Population in UP as Percentage of Total Population in UP

Year	*1951*	*1961*	*1971*	*1981*	*1991*	*2001*
Percentage	13.7	12.9	14.0	18.0	19.8	20.7

Source: Census of India, Different Years.

The rate of urbanization in UP by percentage of settled population was always lower than that for all-India. The percentage gap widened over the fifty years of planned development (1951-2001). If urbanization shows the possibilities of movement of population from rural region, then UP shows lesser possibilities relative to all-India because of high rate of 'local confinement of village settled people' in UP (Majumder, 2005).

The cities in UP, each having settled population more than ten lakhs following Census 2001, are nine in total that account for 42.77 per cent of total urban population in UP. The city of Allahabad accounts for 3.52 per cent of total urban population in UP (Table 3).

Table 3 Population of Cities and Urban Agglomerations in UP

(Total and as % of Urban Population)

Sl. No.	*City/Nagar Nigam*	*Population, 2001*	*Percentage Concentration of Urban Population in UP, 2001*
1.	Kanpur	2772212	8.03
2.	Lucknow	2342289	6.79
3.	Ghaziabad	1815981	5.26
4.	Agra	1557345	4.51
5.	Meerut	1457094	4.22
6.	Varanasi	1268522	3.68
7.	Allahabad	1213828	3.52
8.	Bareily	1172874	3.39
9.	Moradabad	1163478	3.37
	Total	14763623	42.77

Source: Census of India, 2001, Series I.

II. Forced Labour: Rickshaw Pullers in Allahabad City

Most of the population of both working and non-working ages (children and aged) in the countries like India depends on agriculture for mere survival. Even when they report being engaged in non-agricultural activities, these are locally confined with limited mobility and linked with land. In a large country like India by size of total population, and hence population in the working age, this means absence of any choice for the individuals in families other than being dependent on land.

There is, however, no single work for many of the workers. This is not to be read as diversification of jobs that a worker chooses to perform. There is, in fact, no choice for the worker other than trying to minimize the vulnerability by maximizing the number of days she gets the opportunity to work. This work opportunity is also not always clear unless she moves in a state of uncertainty to offer her skill anywhere.

In localized economies of countries like India family bondage works more than the mobility of the individual in the working age. The family as a whole provides income security. It is a collective/ accommodative economy where family priorities come ahead of the individual's self-priorities. Decisions on migration fit in this frame. Often people settled locally (village) move in a state of limited knowledge about job opportunities. This limited knowledge is derived from past practices of the same individual or the practices of her past generation, or the information provided by the local mobile neighbours and friends and relatives. The small underdeveloped locality (village) offers limited social safety and insignificant economic safety. The individual, depending on the socio-cultural characteristics of both the localities 'moving out' and 'moving in', moves with and without families. The 'twin localities' show scope for work for the 'moved out' and 'moved in' individual. While the society-cum-culture works as bondage for the individual, non-development of the local economy drives the individual out. The individual moved out thus may become an economic individual when she 'moves in' to an economic job elsewhere. In most of the cases for the marginalized sections of the locally settled people, it is the survival instinct of the individuals and families that matter in taking decisions regarding economic activities, often under compulsions (Majumder, 2004, p. 623-625).

Based on a study of rickshaw pullers pulling rickshaws in the city of Allahabad, Uttar Pradesh, we found that on average two to three rickshaw pullers pull a rickshaw per day. The average number of rickshaw pullers per year in the city during the last five years (2000-05) came to be 39,228. It means in a small city with

Table 4 Distribution of Rickshaws and Rickshaw Pullers of Allahabad City (2000 – 2005)

Years	*Rickshaws*			*Rickshaw Pullers*			*Rickshaw Pullers per Rickshaw*
	No. of Registered	*Annual Growth*	*Registration Fee*	*Numbers*	*Annual Growth*	*License Fee*	
2000-01	13550	-	159.00	49610	-	20.00	3.66
2001-02	14233	5.04	159.00	45820	-7.63	20.00	3.22
2002-03	15240	7.08	159.00	37329	-18.53	20.00	2.45
2003-04	15472	1.5	160.00	31569	-15.43	20.00	2.04
2004-05	14099	-8.87	160.00	31812	0.77	20.00	2.25
Average	14519	-	-	39228	-	-	2.24

Source: Nagar Nigam, Allahabad.

population around 10.4 lakhs, one rickshaw puller aims at around 26 passengers on any day. This is for the settled population in the city. However, passenger-rickshaw puller ratio depends not essentially on settled population, but more on mobile population who move in and move out of the city for different purposes (Table 4).

(III) Rickshaw Pullers by Occupations, Land Holding, and Income

To understand the nature of forced labour with rickshaw pullers as a case, we looked into the indicators like income, occupations and land holding of the rickshaw pullers. In addition, we looked into the type of influx of population from areas remote from the study zone. We took a sample of fifty rickshaw pullers. We found that most of the rickshaw pullers (60%) pulling rickshaws in the city of Allahabad have their roots in UP, 14 % of them have come from MP, 10 % from Bihar, 12 % from West Bengal, 2 % each from Rajasthan and Jharkhand (Table 5).

Table 5 Distribution of Rickshaw Pullers by Region

State	*Total*	
	No.	***%***
Madhya Pradesh	7	14.0
Uttar Pradesh	30	60.0
Bihar	5	10.0
Jharkhand	1	2.0
West Bengal	6	12.0
Rajasthan	1	2.0
Total	50	100.0

Source: Field Survey 2005.

Occupational Structure

The distribution of main occupations of the households of the rickshaw pullers shows non-agricultural labour as the main occupation for 50.0 per cent of the rickshaw pullers. For 20.0 per cent, the main occupation is cultivation. For only 8.0 per cent, rickshaw pulling is the main occupation. For a few others, occupations like carpentry, basket making, and masonry are the main occupations. Rickshaw pulling, thus, shows support income for 92.0 per cent of the households of the rickshaw pullers. Non-agricultural labour happens to be the main occupation for all. Thus, the households of the rickshaw pullers mainly draw their livelihood from agriculture and non-agricultural labour. Rickshaw pulling remains a support base (Table 6).

Table 6 Main Occupations of Households of Rickshaw Pullers

Occupations	*Total*	
	No.	*%*
Cultivator	10	20.0
Agricultural labour	5	10.0
Non-agricultural labour	25	50.0
Service	1	2.0
Rickshaw Pulling	4	8.0
Carpentry	2	4.0
Mason	1	2.0
Basket Making	2	4.0
Total	50	100.0

Source: Field Survey 2005.

The distribution of main occupations shows that most of the households of rickshaw pullers are engaged as non-agricultural labour (50.0 per cent). The other occupations include agriculture (cultivation and agricultural labour), carpentry, masonry, and basket making. For the households from Bihar, Jharkhand, and Rajasthan, rickshaw pulling is not the main occupation. Of all the rickshaw pullers from UP in the sample, that constitutes 60.0 per cent of total sample, most (50.0 per cent) are mainly engaged as non-agricultural labourers.

Table 7. Main Occupations of Households of Rickshaw Pullers

(By Regions)

Occupation	*MP*		*UP*		*Bihar*		*Jharkhand*		*West Bengal*		*Rajasthan*		*Total*	
	No.	*%*	*No.*	*%*	*No.*	*%*	*No.*	*%*	*No.*	*%*	*No.*	*%*	*No.*	*%*
Cultivator	1	14.3	7	23.3	2	40.0	-	-	-	-	-	-	10	20.0
Agricultural Labour	3	42.8	1	3.3	-	-	1	100.0	-	-	-	-	5	10.0
Non-Agricultural Labour	2	28.6	15	50.0	2	40.0	-	-	5	83.3	1	100.0	25	50.0
Service	-	-	1	3.3	-	-	-	-	-	-	-	-	1	2.0
Rickshaw Pulling	1	14.3	2	6.6	-	-	-	-	1	16.7	-	-	4	8.0
Carpentry	-	-	1	3.3	1	20.0	-	-	-	-	-	-	2	4.0
Masonry	-	-	1	3.3	-	-	-	-	-	-	-	-	1	2.0
Basket making	-	-	2	6.6	-	-	-	-	-	-	-	-	2	4.0
Total	7	100.0	30	100.0	5	100.0	1	100.0	6	100.0	1	100.0	50	100.0

Source: Field Survey 2005.

For the migrant rickshaw pullers from MP, the major household occupations are agricultural labour and non-agricultural labour. Generally for the migrant rickshaw pullers, income-support bases like masonry, carpentry, basket making etc. are absent. For migrants from West Bengal and Rajasthan, even agricultural occupations are absent as main occupations for the households. Thus, the migrants, with the exception of MP, either get engaged in non-agricultural occupations and/or migrate to come to cities like Allahabad to pull rickshaws. Though the small sample size may not show a firm conclusion as such, the fact remains that initial income-poverty and hence necessity to have support income drive people out to search for jobs like rickshaw pulling (Table 7).

As informed by the rickshaw pullers, the only occupational skill that they have is rickshaw pulling. The fact is that the rickshaw pullers as households are engaged in a number of main occupations like non-agricultural labour (50.0 %), carpentry (4.0 %), agricultural labour (10.0 %), cultivation (2.0 %), basket making (4.0 %) etc., in addition to rickshaw pulling. Rickshaw pulling is the main occupation for only 8.0 per cent of the households of the rickshaw pullers. The traditional occupations of the households of rickshaw pullers include carpentry, basket making, carpet/dari weaving etc. It is 'income-support-system' that works through forced participation of the vulnerable sections of the society in a number of main and supplementary occupations. Generally it is 'forced participation' as opposed to 'diversified jobs' (Table 8).

The main occupations of the population from the sample reveal that rickshaw pulling is the main source of income for most. This is natural because the sample is constituted by rickshaw pullers. There are also activities that support family income like cultivation, agricultural and non-agricultural labour, small business, traditional work, driving vehicles (not rickshaw), pulling trolleys, service, animal husbandry etc. In some occupations we found female participation, like cultivation, non-agricultural labour, traditional work, and bidi works. Pulling rickshaws, trolleys, and driving remain a male job.

Table 8. Main and Traditional Occupations and Skill of Rickshaw Pullers

Occupations	*Main Occupations of Households*		*Traditional Occupations of Households*		*Occupational skill of Rickshaw Pullers*	
	No.	*%*	*No.*	*%*	*No.*	*%*
Cultivator	1	2.0	-	-	-	-
Agricultural Labour	5	10.0	-	-	-	-
Non-Agricultural Labour	25	50.0	-	-	-	-
Service	1	2.0	-	-	-	-
Rickshaw Pulling	4	8.0	-	-	49	98.0
Carpet/Dari weaving	-	-	2	4.0	-	-
Bhujai	-	-	1	2.0	-	-
Carpenter	2	4.0	1	2.0	-	-
Mason	1	2.0	-	-	1	2.0
Basket making	2	4.0	2	4.0	-	-
Total	50	100.0	50	100.0	50	100.0

Note: 'Dari' means rope.

Source: Field Survey 2005.

Only 12.67 per cent of the population from the sample reported supplementary occupations. Non-agricultural labour and cultivation cover most of those occupations. We also found agricultural labour, hawking and traditional work. Rickshaw pulling as a source of households' income is reported to be inadequate for survival. The rickshaw pullers need to support their income by other occupations (Table 9).

Table 9 Supplementary Occupations of Sample Population
(By Gender)

Occupations	*Gender*	*Total*
Cultivator	Male	8
	Female	3
	Total	11
Agricultural Labour	Female	1
	Total	1
Non-Agricultural Labour	Male	20
	Female	1
	Total	21
Traditional Work	Female	1
	Total	1
Khatal Business	Male	1
	Total	1
Hawker	Male	1
	Total	1
House Wives	Female	14
	Total	14
No Work	Male	85
	Female	93
	Total	178
Not Applicable	Male	32
	Female	24
	Total	56
Total Male	148	
	Female	136
Total	284	

Note: 'Khatal' means some rickshaws arranged in a particular location.
Source: Field survey 2005.

Income of Population from Sample Households

The range of variation in reported (estimated) income per month of the population from the sample is very high. 8.8 per cent of the population reported income in the range Rs. 500.00 to Rs. 1000.00 p.m. 7.39 per cent of the population earns income per month between Rs. 2000.00 and Rs. 2500.00. Excepting two individuals, all the population in the sample earns income per month below Rs. 4500.00. Of the earning population, 92.47 per cent fall in the monthly income bracket from Rs. 500.00 to Rs. 3000.00.

Of the total male population (148), 52.02 per cent are earners, while of the female population (136), 11.76 per cent are earners. The female earners are only from very low income earning bracket (below Rs. 1000.00 p.m.) (Table 10).

Table 10 Income of Population from Sample per Month

Income (in Rs.)	*Total*		
	Male	*Female*	*Total*
Below 500	3	8	11
500-1000	9	8	17
1001-1500	11	-	11
1501-2000	17	-	17
2001-2500	21	-	21
2501-3000	12	-	12
3001-4500	2	-	2
8000	1	-	1
12000	1	-	1
Non-Earning	71	120	191
Total	148	136	284

Source: Field survey 2005.

The earning population from the sample earn on average Rs. 1900.00 per month. This is weighted average monthly income over all earning population that covers monthly income as low as below Rs. 1000.00 and as high as above Rs. 8000.00. The average income per month of male population from SCs is Rs. 2024.00, which is Rs. 2176.00 covering all caste categories. The average income per month of female population is Rs. 572.00. Female income of the earning population from the sample of rickshaw pullers, thus, is much less than the male income.

Table 11. Average Monthly Income of Households of Rickshaw Pullers

Income (in Rs.)	*Particulars*	*Total*
Below 1500	Number	1
	PHHMI	1200
1500 to 2000	Number	8
	PHHMI	1950
2001 to 2500	Number	9
	PHHMI	2444
2501 to 3000	Number	9
	PHHMI	2966
3001 to 4000	Number	9
	PHHMI	3644
4001 to 5000	Number	7
	PHHMI	4557
5001 to 6000	Number	2
	PHHMI	5530
6001 to 8000	Number	4
	PHHMI	7250
Above 8000	Number	1
	PHHMI	17000
Total	Number	50
	PHHMI	3745
Per Capita Monthly Income		659
Average Family Size		5.7

Note: PHHMI = Per Household monthly Income in Rupees.

Source: Field survey 2005

The average income per household per month generally varies between Rs. 1500.00 and Rs. 5000.00. This range covers as high as 84.0 per cent of the rickshaw pullers. 18.0 per cent of the rickshaw pullers fall in each of the income bracket, between Rs. 2000.00 and Rs. 2500.00, between Rs. 2500.00 and Rs. 3000.00, between Rs. 3000.00 and Rs. 4000.00. Thus, there is wide range of variations in monthly income per household for even middle-income bracket (Rs. 2000.00 to Rs. 4000.00) that covers 54.0 per cent of the rickshaw pullers. Generally, thus, income per month per household varies between Rs. 2000.00 and Rs. 4000.00 for most of the rickshaw pullers (Table 11).

Land Holding Pattern

Of all the rickshaw pullers migrating to the city of Allahabad from within UP, 56.66 per cent are landless; 80.0 per cent migrating from Bihar are landless, 83.33 per cent from West Bengal are landless, which is 57.14 per cent for MP. Of all the sample rickshaw pullers, 64.0 per cent are landless. Excepting 13.33 per cent of the rickshaw pullers migrating from within UP, no one owns agricultural land more than 3.0 acres. Excepting two rickshaw pullers from UP and one from Bihar, no one owns agricultural land above 2.0 acres. Landlessness and marginal landholding (less than 2.0 acres) is a major factor to drive the population out from the root. These people become rootless when they are forced to migrate to a city like Allahabad to pull rickshaws (Table 12).

36.0 per cent of the rickshaw pullers own agricultural land. Of those having agricultural land, 72.2 per cent are from UP. The average landholding for those in UP having land is 1.79 acre. For MP this average is 0.75 acre, West Bengal 1.26 acre, Bihar 2.52 acre. The area cultivated remains less than the area owned for this migrating population. On average, total cultivated land as percentage of total agricultural land owned by the migrating rickshaw pullers remains 67.02. The small average agricultural landholding, and smaller cultivated land, forced people to move out to the city like Allahabad to be drawn into rickshaw pulling.

Table 12 Distribution of Households based on Size of Agricultural Land Holding

(In Acres)

States	*Landless*		*Up to 0.5*		*0.5 – 1.0*		*1.0 – 2.0*		*2.0 – 3.0*		*3.0 – 4.0*		*Total*	
	No.	*%*	*No.*	*%*	*No.*	*%*	*No.*	*%*	*No.*	*%*	*No.*	*%*	*No.*	*%*
Madhya Pradesh	4	12.5	-	-	3	60.0	-	-	-	-	-	-	7	14.0
Uttar Pradesh	17	53.1	3	100.0	2	40.0	2	66.7	2	66.7	4	100.0	30	60.0
Bihar	4	12.5	-	-	-	-	-	-	1	33.3	-	-	5	10.0
Jharkhand	1	3.1	-	-	-	-	-	-	-	-	-	-	1	2.0
West Bengal	5	15.6	-	-	-	-	1	33.3	-	-	-	-	6	12.0
Rajasthan	1	3.1	-	-	-	-	-	-	-	-	-	-	1	2.0
Total	32	100.0	3	100.0	5	100.0	3	100.0	3	100.0	4	100.0	50	100.0

Source: Field Survey 2005.

(IV) Migration: Reasons

The rickshaw pullers in the city of Allahabad had been involved in a number of jobs before they joined rickshaw pulling. These jobs were cultivation, agricultural labour, non-agricultural labour, traditional work, domestic service, masonry, driving, bidi making, basket making, trolley pulling etc. Most of them (30.0 per cent) were engaged as non-agricultural labourers; 26.0 per cent were engaged as agricultural labourers; 28.0 per cent as cultivators; only 8.0 per cent were previously engaged as rickshaw pullers before they entered into Allahabad for the same job. 20.0 per cent of the rickshaw pullers were unemployed/ not-engaged in any productive activities before joining the job of rickshaw pulling in the city of Allahabad. There are regional variations in the distribution of past occupations of the people who migrated to the city of Allahabad to be rickshaw pullers.

The reasons why the rickshaw pullers gave up the past occupations include factors like income, health, distance, nature of job and company, superannuation, accident, social respect, natural calamities etc. Most of the rickshaw pullers are not involved in occupations other than pulling rickshaws. Most of those who seek other jobs are from within UP for support income, or enhancement of family income. 26.0 per cent of the rickshaw pullers get also involved in wage work. Of those who get involved in wage work, 76.92 per cent are from UP. The other kinds of jobs that the rickshaw pullers do include 'working under contractor' (casual labour), working as a vendor (selling vegetables, fish, and fruits), wage work in hotels, and wage labour (part time) in hotels. Thus, the rickshaw pullers depend mainly on pulling rickshaws. The other jobs, if available, supplement their family income. Of the rickshaw pullers whose root is in the state of UP, the district Allahabad is the root for 60.0 per cent, the rest have migrated from near and remote districts like Banda and Chitrakoot in the Bundelkhand region, from districts like Pratapgarh, Balia, Kaushambi, Raibareli, Jaunpur, and Fatehpur in east UP. Thus, the rickshaw pullers migrated from relatively underdeveloped regions like east UP and Bundelkhand, and not from relatively better off regions like west and central UP.

The reasons behind the involuntarily entry into the job of rickshaw pulling were non-existence of any choice (no alternative job available); lower income in other jobs (related to expected income in rickshaw pulling); no capital (money) to be self-employed, long distance between place of stay and place of work, and discarded by family.

(V) Rickshaw Pulling: Forced Labour or Self-exploitation?

How can the job of rickshaw pulling be forced in nature when the pullers are self-employed, whether or not they own the rickshaws? Does it mean self-exploitation?

As we observed, the pullers joined the job of pulling in a condition of helplessness, which is 'involuntary employment'. The very little income from the major sources or occupation forces the people to search for alternative jobs for support income. In absence of any skill required in the formal (organized sector) and/or the organized sector itself being small relative to socially required labour-capital ratios, the shifted/migrated people join jobs like rickshaw pulling. Often for some this job becomes the major source of family income. However, for most of the households of the sample rickshaw pullers, agriculture and related activities (including non-agricultural job in rural region) show major sources of income.

It is not working with dignity that attracts potential workers to join the job of rickshaw pulling. The pullers do not work under any roof, in a particular time frame, that could ensure their better living-cum-working condition. The rickshaw pullers seem to decide their own working hours. However, reducing working hours per day means for him proportionate reducing income, and saving (after payment of rent etc.). The puller can not afford to do this. Hence, the puller exploits self. Family responsibility reinforces this self-exploitation.

For the marginalized people living below the line of biological existence, rational choice is never a determining factor to get engaged in economic occupations. The occupations where these people can expect to enter into are in the informal sector of the economy. Rickshaw pulling is a category where the pullers are expected to run rickshaws purely manually. For those having very little cultivable land holding the job supports family income often to be meant for repaying old debt or fulfilling family rituals for social benefits at personal/family cost. For those having no cultivable land in the village, the alternative opportunity cost is zero, implying no choice but to surrender in the labour market. Labour remains expendable.

The first job may be choice-neutral. However, the worker will have either acquired competence in the said initial job or satisfied in the job (by relations with other workers in the same job and with the buyers of the service) or searches to change the job. In case of most of the so-called diversified jobs for the marginalized workers, the choices of changing jobs do not exist from the demand side. These workers are often forced to think about new jobs or are drawn into other jobs. Local labour contractors often do this. In other words, the workers in the job of rickshaw pulling generally have no breathing space to think about other jobs, even if those jobs exist. Getting shifted from one job today to another job tomorrow may not really show the mobility of the workers. Mobility in the informal sector for the marginalized sections of the workers is a misnomer.

Pulling rickshaws is a choice under compulsion. Often it aims at supporting family income. It is so far only a male job anywhere in India and like countries. Thus, generally the male individuals leave the root and family for a short or medium period and come to city either with knowledge about their chance to get rickshaws to pull, or get rickshaws to pull under circumstances not known earlier. Because of many reasons, pulling rickshaws may not be a choice for the pullers for an indefinite period.

Since most of the rickshaw pullers pulling rickshaws provide support income for the family, hence the pullers do not continue to search for other employment opportunities. This is true particularly for those migrating from rural (agriculture or land-based occupations) regions for whom 'local' occupation (agriculture or land-based occupations) provides major income and attachment. Off-season migration for some and job-less forced migration for others push male people out to come to city to join the job of rickshaw pulling. A calculation of alternative opportunity cost (that could show shift from rickshaw pulling to higher order jobs) do not carry much meaning, excepting for some who can shift to higher paid full time jobs, or can open up small business etc. The rickshaw pullers in a small city like Allahabad remain rational by 'choice under economic compulsions' in accepting and remaining stable in rickshaw pulling.

(VI) Suggestions

Rickshaw pulling shows the extreme level of labour intensity. We suggest the following measures that may provide some temporary relief to the rickshaw pullers (on the assumption that rickshaw pulling remains in practice):

- The competent development authority of the city/town should allot cluster-type living space for rickshaw pullers along with the scope to keep the rickshaws that they own/run ,

- The city development authority is used to take license fee for both rickshaw and puller, so that it becomes the responsibility of the authority to fix location for rickshaw stands. The guiding indicator for such fixation may be the conventional (existing) locations where mostly the rickshaw pullers wait to pull rickshaws in the city.

- It is necessary to link rickshaw pullers with other alternative job opportunities (through vocational training for tailoring/ weaving, small shops, cottage industry, etc.). The city as well as District Urban Development Authority (DUDA) should take the responsibility to identify the rickshaw pullers who have been pulling rickshaws for more than five years continuously in the city, and encompass them in the training net.

- The city development authority must stop providing license to those rickshaw pullers who are below 18 years and above 65 years.

- The city development authority should chalk out plan for rehabilitation with pension of old (say, above age 65) rickshaw pullers in proportion with the period of rickshaw pulling with the minimum duration of ten years.

- The district labour department should form a 'Welfare Association' for rickshaw pullers and strengthen it in terms of education, health, sanitation and awareness of rickshaw pullers' children so that the children may be prohibited to enter into this job.

- The city development authority may link rickshaw pullers with local financial institutions to provide either rickshaws or to provide equivalent interest free loans to purchase rickshaws with state guarantee for loan repayment over a stipulated period.

- In case one rickshaw is drawn by more than one puller, the city development authority may encourage cooperative type organization for joint ownership-cum-maintenance of rickshaws.

References

Breman, Jan, 1996, 'Footloose Labour, Working in India's Informal Economy', Cambridge Univ. Press.

Harris-White, Barbara, 2004, 'India Working, Essays on Society and Economy', Cambridge Univ. Press.

Majumder, Bhaskar, 2004, 'Informalization of Global Labour and Survival of Local Workers', Productivity, Vol. 44, No. 4, Jan-March.

————————, 2004a, 'Living in Slums: A Study of the City of Allahabad, Uttar Pradesh', Mimeo, G. B. Pant Social Science Institute, Allahabad, India.

————————, 2005, 'Rural Housing and Living Condition of People Settled in Rural Uttar Pradesh: A Study', Report submitted to Planning Commission, Government of India.

11

Rootlessness of Labour: A Study of the Rickshaw Pullers of the City of Allahabad

An individual becomes a worker by doing any job/work independent of the time rule (labour hour) and collects/produces products for herself (including her family). The worker always exists as a social category, while labour exists as an economic category. Capitalism converts a worker into a labourer willing to sell labour power (a commodity) to the buyer (another individual or owner/collector of non-labour resources) at the prevailing (or agreed upon) price (wage rate). Labour (hour) becomes the root or cause of all products, that is the time expression of labour power embedded in a labourer. The labour hour gets concrete shape in products and services. Institutions convert a social category into an economic category, and hence a worker becomes a 'labourer'. An individual starts working in paid job (wage-employment) independent of his own will, and dependent on prevailing laws, customs, practices etc., as shown by institutions. In absence of any laws for the workers, the labour market remains informal, that is, where workers operate without written accounts and labour contracts. Most of these workers in the informal sector are self-employed, often assisted by unpaid family workers. Following ILO, the informal sector excludes agriculture for practical reasons. The workers are self-employed in the informal sector in the sense that they directly receive the rewards of their labour (ILO, 2000, p. 194).

The present study deals with the case of rickshaw pullers where the very joining the job is involuntary, in the sense that it happens in a condition of helplessness. Tips and income characterize what these workers earn by piece-rates by coverage of a specific distance. The workers are mostly employed by the owners of rickshaws but not paid by the latter. In this sense, the rickshaw pullers show some exceptions to the concept of self-employment. However, they confirm the ILO definition by receiving income directly from those whom they provide service.

The paper focuses on 'forced labour' that reflects rootlessness of people waiting in the queue to be workers. 'Forced' labour is mainly an urban phenomenon, when the worker feels compelled (forced) to leave the root (village and land-linked activities), at least temporarily, to migrate to urban region in search of 'any' job to earn 'support income'.

This paper has seven sections. In Section I we briefly narrate the urbanization-related inflow and exodus of people. In Section II we analyze the nature of occupation and labour of 'locality'. In Section III we offer the objectives, methodology, coverage and sample of the study. In Section IV we deal with the nature of 'rootlessness' or so-called migration of people considered as labourers with rickshaw pullers as a case. In Section V we cite a specific example of 'survival instinct' of rootless labourers, that is, of the rickshaw pullers. Section VI deals with the nature of 'rootlessness' or self-exploitation. Finally, in Section VII we offer concluding comments.

Urbanization: Inflow and Exodus of People

Urbanization is known as a process of agglomeration of population that gets settled within a narrow boundary relative to the size of settled population showing high density of population per square kilometer. Natural increase in population, shift of existing urban boundary, and reclassification of areas known earlier as villages lead to formation of towns/cities. Composition of towns/ cities shows urban regions.

The offshoot of urbanization will be reflected in net migration of population in a frame of rural-urban inflows and outflows of population, setting up of industries in urban boundaries, increasing percentage of population waiting at the gates of the industries, deruralization, and formation of both formal and informal labour market with increasing reserve army of labourers. In conventional literature, urbanization is measured by certain parameters like density of population, percentage of population engaged in secondary and tertiary occupations, production of land-delinked goods, improved infrastructure, easy communication, etc.

A particular location may be attractive to some individuals to use the location economically and hence attract population for ultimate settlement. These locations may be resource rich, linked by railways, by ports etc and hence become the centre of attraction for at least economic purposes. Movement of people from the periphery is a corollary. The probability of getting jobs, wage-differential and hence higher standard of living, better education and health act as a 'pitcher plant' in the urban economy (Majumder, 2004). A city is a constituent of this urban economy.

The carrying capacity and vibrancy of a city is understood by the size of the settled population in a city, the quality of the people in terms of understanding the scope and nature of work, and the actual frequency of people moving in and moving out. This, at the same time, shows mobility of workers in search of economic occupations. That a city is economically attractive is partially proved by the influx while the exodus shows the search for outside jobs by some of the settled people. For a city that can attract people from outside, it will be prima facie difficult to understand why people move out. One reason could be wage-differential, while there may also be non-economic parameters like heredity-cum-caste determined jobs, prevalence of caste division of labour etc. Potential workers settled inside the city may be reluctant to be engaged in a particular type of job because of cultural taboo.

We are concerned in this study on influx of people from outside the city. This influx covers a geographic distance that is both short and long. The 'short-distance' influx is generally characterized by 'easy come, easy go' like entering into the city in the morning and going back at the end of the same day or at the end of the week. The long-distance influx is 'long-stay' type associated with going home after money/saving is accumulated. The circulation of labour by periodic migration has been elaborately recorded in the context of south Gujarat elsewhere (Breman, 1996).

Nature of Occupation and Labour of Locality

Because of push and pull factors, the population gets settled in urban region. Though in a primarily land (agriculture) dependent economy people would prefer to remain locally confined, economic compulsions often make them unsettled. This unsettlement leads to migration of many types including 'forced' one. Urbanization is a consequence of both voluntary and forced migration of settled population from earlier settled village economy.

Most of the population of both working and non-working ages (children and aged) in the countries like India depends on agriculture for mere survival. Even when they report being engaged in non-agricultural activities, these are locally confined with limited mobility and linked with land. In a large country like India by size of total population, and hence population in the working age, this means absence of any choice for the individuals in families other than being dependent on land. There is, however, no single work for many of the workers. This is not to be read as diversification of jobs that a worker chooses to perform. There is, in fact, no choice for the worker other than trying to minimize the vulnerability by maximizing the number of days she gets the opportunity to work. This work opportunity is also not always clear unless she moves in a state of uncertainty to offer her skill anywhere.

In localized economies of countries like India family bondage works more than the mobility of the individual in the working age. The family as a whole provides income security. It is a collective/ accommodative economy where family priorities come ahead of the individual's self-priorities. Decisions of migration fit in this frame. Often people settled locally (village) move in a state of limited knowledge about job opportunities. This limited knowledge is derived from past practices of the same individual or the practices of her past generations, or the information provided by the local mobile neighbours and friends and relatives. The small underdeveloped locality (village) offers limited social safety and insignificant economic safety. The individual, depending on the socio-cultural characteristics of both the localities 'moving out' and 'moving in', moves with and without families. The 'twin localities' show scope for work for the 'moved out' and 'moved in' individual. While the society-cum-culture works as bondage for the individual, non-development of the local economy drives the individual out. The individual moved out thus may become an economic individual when she 'moves in' to an economic job elsewhere. In most of the cases for the marginalized sections of the locally settled people, it is the survival instinct of the individuals and families that matter in taking decisions regarding economic activities, often under compulsions.

Objectives, Methodology, Coverage and Sample for the Study

Recently we conducted a study on the nature of labour in the informal sector taking rickshaw pullers as a case (Majumder, 2005). The study was exploratory aimed at unearthing the roots and reasons for migration of workers to ultimately work as rickshaw pullers. The study zone was the city of Allahabad including its outskirts in Uttar Pradesh, India. The city has five administrative regions in terms of direction, namely, east, west north, south, and central. We took a sample of 50 rickshaw pullers distributed equally over these five regions. In each of the regions within the city of Allahabad, we covered as far as practicable all the 'mohallas' (colony) where the rickshaw pullers are settled by residence. In total we covered 40 'mohallas distributed over the five regions 'tolerably equally' (14.0 per cent of 'mohallas' at the minimum to 20.0 per cent at the maximum per region) considered over all the five regions. We also covered eight (08) owners of rickshaws (owners of 'Khatals' known by arrangement of many rickshaws in a particular location). Some of the rickshaw pullers do not stay in the city, who come from adjoining villages. In the sample of fifty rickshaw pullers, the floating/moving pullers are seven in number, or 14.0 percent of total sample rickshaw pullers. Following pilot visit and information from secondary sources (like Allahabad Nagar Nigam), we came to know that there is no proper rickshaw stand in the city, so that the rickshaw pullers choose the major locations or informal rickshaw stands while collecting primary information. By social categories we covered all the castes and communities like the scheduled castes (SC), the other backward castes (OBC), the people in general castes, and the Muslims. We also took care of the rickshaw pullers by their age distribution.

Migration of People: Past Occupations-cum-Ownership over Means of Production

We found that most of the rickshaw pullers (60.0 per cent) pulling rickshaws in the city of Allahabad have their roots in U. P., 14.0 per cent of them have from MP, 10.0 per cent from Bihar and 12.0 per cent from West Bengal, and 2.0 from each of Rajasthan and Jharkhand. The basic reasons why people at the bottom of the economic ladder migrate to other regions are linked with their past/initial occupations and their ownership over means of production. Since these people initially settled in the rural region of an economy are linked with land as the major productive asset, hence we looked into the land holding of the people who migrated to be ultimately the rickshaw pullers in the city of Allahabad.

The distribution of the main occupations shows that most of the households of the rickshaw pullers are engaged as non-agricultural labour (50.0 per cent). The other occupations include agriculture (cultivation and agricultural labour), carpentry, masonry, and basket making. For the households from Bihar, Jharkhand and Rajasthan, rickshaw pulling is the main occupation. Of all the rickshaw pullers from UP in the sample, most (50.0 per cent) are mainly engaged as non-agricultural labourers, seen from households' major occupation point of view.

For the migrant rickshaw pullers from Madhya Pradesh (MP), the major household occupation is agricultural labour and non-agricultural labour. Generally for the migrant rickshaw pullers, income-support bases like works of a mason, carpentry, basket making are absent. For migrant from West Bengal and Rajasthan, even agricultural occupations are absent as main occupations for the households. Thus, the migrants, with the exception of MP, either get engaged in non-agricultural occupations and/or migrate to cities like Allahabad to pull rickshaws. Initial income-poverty and hence necessity to have support income drives people out to search for jobs like rickshaw pulling.

The distribution of main occupations of the population from the sample reveals that rickshaw pulling is the main source of income for most of the pullers. This is natural because rickshaw pullers constitute our sample. There are also activities that support family income like cultivation, agricultural and non-agricultural labour, small business, traditional work, driving vehicles other than rickshaws, pulling trolleys, service, animal husbandry, etc. In some occupations we found female participation, like cultivation, non-agricultural labour, traditional work, and bidi works. Pulling rickshaws, trolleys, and driving remains a male job.

Only 12.67 per cent of the population from the sample reported supplementary occupations. Non-agricultural labour and cultivation cover most of those occupations. We also found agricultural labour, hawking and traditional work. Thus, rickshaw pulling as a source of households' income is reported to be inadequate for survival. The rickshaw pullers need to enhance their income by other occupations.

Most of the rickshaw pullers are not involved in occupations other than pulling rickshaws. Most of those who seek other jobs are from within UP for enhancement of family income. 26.0 per cent of the rickshaw pullers get also involved in wage work, 76.92 per cent are from UP. The other kinds of jobs that the rickshaw pullers do include 'working under contractor' (casual labour), working as vendor (selling vegetables, fish, and fruits), and wage labour (part time) in hotels. The rickshaw pullers depend mainly on pulling rickshaws for income. The other jobs, if available, supplement their family income.

Of all the sample rickshaw pullers, 64.0 per cent are landless. Of the entire rickshaw pullers migrating to the city of Allahabad from within UP, 56.66 per cent are landless; 80 per cent from Bihar are landless, 83.33 per cent from West Bengal are landless, while it is 57.14 per cent for MP. Except for 13.33 per cent of the rickshaw pullers migrating from within UP, no one owns agriculture land more than 3.0 acres. Excepting two rickshaw pullers from UP and one from Bihar, no owns agricultural land above 2.0 acres. Landlessness and marginal landholding (less than 2.0 acre) is a major factor to drive the population out from the root. These people become rootless when they are forced to migrate.

Of all the rickshaw pullers who are settled in the state of UP, the district of Allahabad is the root for 60.0 per cent, the rest have migrated from near and remote districts like Banda and Chitrakoot in the Bundelkhand region, from districts like Pratapgarh, Balia, Kaushambi, Raibareli, Jaunpur and Fatehpur in east UP. In our sample, thus, the rickshaw pullers migrated from relatively underdeveloped regions like east UP and Bundelkhand, and not from relatively better off regions like west and central UP. We, however, did not find any direct link between underdevelopment of a region and out-migration. Only 14.0 per cent of the rickshaw pullers in the city of Allahabad do not stay in the city and go back to the adjoining villages at the end of the day. As high as 40.0 per cent of the pullers stay alone in the city, while 26.0 per cent stay with family in the city. The rest manage to stay with other rickshaw pullers, 'known relatives' staying in the city since past, etc.

Excepting one rickshaw puller who migrated from Rajasthan to the city of Allahabad and started pulling rickshaws, others are in the habit of moving in and moving out (work place to living place) by different time gaps. In the sample, for 16.0 per cent of the rickshaw pullers, the movement is indefinite; 20.0 per cent of the pullers go home once in a quarter; 18.0 per cent go fortnightly, 14.0 per cent go monthly; 10.0 per cent go yearly. The rest come from the adjoining villages and hence commute daily. The rickshaw pullers, thus, maintain links with native places by their movements with varying frequency. The only migrant from Jharkhand moves once in a month while of all migrants from Bihar, it is a movement either quarterly or yearly. There is no state-specificity in movements of rickshaw pullers by specific frequency. The fact is that the rickshaw pullers generally maintain links with their roots even after they had migrated.

Survival Instinct of Rootless Labourers: Less Rootlessness

We estimated from the responses of the sample rickshaw pullers that the range of variation of their income per day per person is Rs. 60.00 at the minimum to Rs. 150.00 at the maximum. In addition to the observed fact that the rickshaw pullers live in a hostile social environment, it remains a question how do they survive. The relevance of the question comes from the fact that the rickshaw pullers at the bottom of the economic ladder are already in debt because of money borrowed and spent to shoulder family responsibilities and socio-cultural compulsions.

On average a rickshaw puller pulls rickshaw for 20/25 days a month. Most of the rickshaw pullers do not own rickshaws. They take these on rent. The rent that each pays on average to the owner of the rickshaw varies between Rs. 15 and Rs. 25 per day per rickshaw, depending on the condition of the rickshaw, old or new. The minor maintenance/repair cost is borne by the puller. In the expectation of raising real income by saving (both cash and kind), the rickshaw pullers innovate strategies. We found one such strategy in the city of Allahabad. The strategy is sharing food in community kitchen.

We observed in the Kareli area in central Allahabad the community kitchens for the rickshaw pullers. These kitchens, meant for serving food only to the rickshaw pullers, serve multi-purposes for them. It is a single katcha room made of clothes, straw, paper, plastic and some clay materials. Inside the room there are both 'chulla' (indigenous oven) and ceiling fan somehow fixed. We found a number of such kitchens in the identified area.

The rickshaw pullers get cheap food in these kitchens run by women. It runs on a daily basis. The rickshaw pullers take food in the morning in the kitchen before they go out to pull rickshaws, come back at around 2-3 p.m. to take mid-day meal following which they take rest inside the same kitchen. The average size of the kitchen-cum-dining space-cum-rest room is around 100 sq. ft. that can accommodate around ten persons. There remains no space between any two persons trying to take rest for a nap. Thus, one person occupies on average six-by-two sq. ft. to sleep/rest. Generally, all the ten persons who on average are supposed to take meal on a day do not eat food at the same time, nor do they take rest at the same time point. They are supposed to do these two activities by turn. After the rickshaw pullers take rest, they go out to pull rickshaws again. Thus, the rickshaw pullers get meal in these community kitchens thrice a day. These kitchens-cum-residences are on a rental basis. The rent per month is Rs. 200 that is paid to the owner of the plot of land. The shed is prepared by the tenant herself/himself. There is no improvement of the shed because, with a notice of ten to fifteen days from the owner of the plot of land, the land may need to be vacated and the tenant will have to shift to some other place.

The rickshaw pullers pay Rs. 20 for all the three meals per day per person, which is cheap by comparison with meals available outside the roadside food stalls. The additional benefit that the rickshaw pullers get in the community kitchens is scope to take rest for some hours covered by the same cost. There is no fixed kitchen for the migrated rickshaw pullers. However, the cost is the same per person per day; it is Rs. 20 for three meals a day. The quantity-cum-items that they take will cost around Rs. 40 per person per day from any roadside food stall in the city of Allahabad. Thus, the rickshaw pullers save (real saving) per day Rs. 20 on food account, so that their real saving comes to be Rs. 600 on food account per month, based on taking food everyday from these community kitchens. The rickshaw pullers who are used to taking meals in these community kitchens migrated from the areas like the Malda district of West Bengal for a reasonable period. They migrated individually, so that the choices are that each one of them cooks alone, or takes food alone from the roadside stalls, or takes collective benefits from the community kitchens. Rationally they choose the last option.

If on average each rickshaw puller earns Rs. 100 per day from the passengers, of which he pays Rs. 25 to the owner of the rickshaw, then each on average is left with Rs. 75 per day. Of this, each pays Rs. 20 to the owner of the community kitchen, so that each is left with Rs. 55 per day. On average, thus, each rickshaw puller can expect to earn Rs. 1650 per month if he pulls rickshaw every day. These rickshaw pullers migrate to such cities as Allahabad for saving cash to take it back home. If a portion of the money is spent on non-food items, say 10.0 per cent, then each rickshaw puller can expect to save approximately Rs. 1500 per month to take back home. This seems to be reasonable in view of non-availability of wage-work for most of the periods at home region. The income-saving calculations show, however, overestimations.

Nature of Rootlessness or Self-Exploitation

As we observed, the rickshaw pullers have joined the job of pulling rickshaws in a condition of helplessness, which shows 'involuntary employment'. The very little income from the major sources or occupation forces the people to search for alternative jobs for support income. In absence of any skill required in the formal (organized sector) and/or the organized sector itself being small relative to socially required labour-capital ratios, the shifted/ migrated people join the job of rickshaw pulling. Often for some this job becomes the major source of family income. However, for most of the households of the sample rickshaw pullers, it is agriculture and related activities (including non-agricultural jobs in rural region) that show major sources of income.

It is not working with dignity that attracts potential workers to join the job of rickshaw pulling. The pullers do not work under any roof, in a particular time frame, that could ensure their better living-cum-working condition. The rickshaw pullers seem to decide their own working hours. However, reducing working hours per day or reducing number of days to pull rickshaws per month means for him proportionate reduction in income and saving. The puller cannot afford to do this. Hence, the puller exploits self. Family responsibility reinforces this self-exploitation.

For the marginalized people living below the line of biological existence, rational choice is never a determining factor to get engaged in economic occupations. Rickshaw pulling is a category where the pullers are expected to run rickshaws purely manually. For those having very little cultivable land holding the job supports family income often to be meant for repaying old debt or fulfilling family rituals for social benefits at personal/family cost.

The first job may be choice-neutral. However, the worker will have either acquired competence in the said initial job (by relations with other workers in the same job and with the buyers of the service) or searches for job changes. In case of most of the so-called diversified jobs for the marginalized workers, the choices of changing jobs do not exist from the demand side. These workers are often forced to think about new jobs or are drawn into other jobs. Local labour contractors often do his. In other works, the workers in the job of rickshaw pulling generally have no breathing space to think about other jobs, even if those jobs exist. Getting shifted from one job today to another job tomorrow may not really show the mobility of the workers. Mobility in the informal sector for the marginalized sections of the workers is a misnomer.

Concluding Comments

Pulling rickshaws is a choice under compulsion. Often it aims at supporting family income. It is so far only a male job. Thus, generally the male individuals leave the root and family for a short or medium term and come to the city either with knowledge about their choice to get rickshaws to pull, or get rickshaws to pull under circumstances not known earlier. Because of many reasons pulling rickshaws may not be a choice for the pullers for an indefinite period.

Since, following our study, most of the rickshaw pullers pulling rickshaws provide support income for the family, hence, the pullers do not continue to search for other emplcyment opportunities. This is true particularly for those migrating from rural (agriculture or land-based occupations) regions for whom 'local' occupation (agricultural or land-based occupations) provides major income and attachment. Off-season migration for some and job-less forced migration for others push male people out to come to city to join the job of rickshaw pulling. The rickshaw pullers in a small city like Allahabad remain rational by 'choice under economic compulsion' in accepting and remaining stable in rickshaw pulling.

Reference

Breman, Jan. (1996). 'Footloose Labour, Working in India's Informal Economy', Cambridge Univ. Press.

ILO. (2000). World Labour Report, Geneva.

Majumdr, Bhaskar. (2004). 'Informalization of Global Labour and Survival of Local Workers', Productivity, Vol. 44, NO. 4, Jan-March.

——————————. (2005). 'Forced Labour: A Study of Rickshaw Pullers of Allahabad City, Uttar Pradesh', Project Report, Mimeo, G. B. Pant Social Science Institute, Allahabad.

Bibliography

Alam, Moneer and Mishra, S. N., (1998), 'Structural Reforms and Employment Issues in India: A Case of Industrial Labour', *The Indian Journal of Labour Economics*, Vol. 41, No. 2, April-June.

Alavi, Hamza (1982), "State and Class under Peripheral Capitalism", in Alavi, H. and T. Shanin, (eds), *Introduction to the Sociology of Developing Societies*, Macmillan.

Banerjee, N. (1988), 'The Unorganized Sector and the Planner' in A.K. Bagchi (Ed), 'Economy, Society and Polity, Essays in the Political Economy of Indian Planning', Oxford University Press, Delhi.

Bardhan, P. (1984), *The Political Economy of Development in India*, Oxford University Press, Delhi.

Bhalla, G. S. (1995), "Globalisation and Agricultural Policy in India", *Indian Journal of Agricultural Economics*, Vol. 50, No. 1. January-March.

Breman, Jan, (2003), "Globalization, Poverty and Exclusion", G. B. Pant Memorial Lecture delivered in G. B. Pant Social Science Institute, Allahabad, Oct. 20-22.

Breman, Jan, 1996, 'Footloose Labour, Working in India's Informal Economy', Cambridge Univ. Press.

Cahan, Jean Axelrad, (1994-95), "The Concept of Property in Marx's Theory of History: A Defence of the Autonomy of the Socio-economic Base", *Science and Society*, Vol. 58, No. 4, Winter.

Census of India (1991), Registrar General and Census Commissioner India, Ministry of Home Affairs, *Primary Census Abstract, Series I, Part II-B(1),* Vol. II. New Delhi.

Chakravarty, S., 1988, 'Development of Development Thinking', Arthavijnana, Vol. XXX, No. 2, June.

Chandra, Ashok, (1999), 'Retraining for Redevelopment: NRF Initiative and Challenge in Training', *The Indian Journal of Labour Economics*, Vol. 42, No. 1, Jan-March.

Dandekar, A.K. (1968), 'India' in Adams, Walter (Ed.) 'The Brain Drain' The Macmillan Company, New York.

Dasgupta, A.K. (1991), 'Foundation and Structure of Real Resource Based Planning for Economic Growth, Seminar (Alternative Manpower Planning Structure(, Paper, IAMR, New Delhi, January 6-7.

DSHA (1998), Economics and Statistics Department, State Planning Institute, *District Statistical Handbook of Allahabad*, Uttar Pradesh.

Fearn, Robert M., (1981), Labour Economies: The Emerging Synthesis, Winthrop Pub. Cambridge.

GOI (1991), *India's New Economic Policies*, Government of India, Ministry of External Affairs, New Delhi.

Gorden, David, M. (1988) 'The Global Economy New Edifice or Crumbling Foundations?', New Left Review, No. 168, March-April.

Griffin, K. and A. R. Khan (1978), "Poverty in the Third World: Ugly Facts and Fancy Models", *World Development*, Vol. 6, No. 3.

Griffin, Keith, (1981), 'Economic Development in a Changing World', World Development, Vol. 9, No. 3, March

Harris-White, Barbara, 2004, 'India Working, Essays on Society and Economy', Cambridge Univ. Press.

Hicks, J. R. (1971), "The Social Framework", Oxford Univ. Press, London.

Hicks, J.R., 1965, 'Capital and Growth', Oxford Univ. Press, London.

ILO (1997-98), *World Labour Report*, Geneva

ILO (1999), *World Employment Report*, Bookwell, Delhi.

ILO, (1974), "Sharing in Development: A Programme of Employment, Equity and Growth for the Philippines", ILO Geneva.

ILO, (1998-99), *World Employment Report*, Geneva

ILO, (2000), "World Labour Report", Geneva.

ILO, (2001), *World Employment Report*, Geneva

International Labour Office (ILO), (1966), Report of the Director General, Part I, International Labour Conference, 50th Session, Geneva.

Kerr, Clark (1954) 'The Balkanization of labour Markets' in Bakke, E.W. et al, 'Labour Mobility and Economic Opportunity', The Technology Press, New York.

Kerr, P., 1993, 'Adam Smith's Theory of Growth and Technological Change', Contributions to Political Economy, Vol. 12.

Kurien, C. T. (1987), "State and Market in Economic Process: Some Basic Issues", *Economic and Political Weekly*, Vol. XXII, Annual Number, May.

Kuznets, S., 1961, Six Lectures on Economic Growth, The Free Press, USA.

Kuznets, S., 1965, Economic Growth and Structure, W.W. Norton And Co., New York.

Lester, Richard A. (1967), 'The Role of Organized Labour', in Gordon, Robert A. (Ed.), 'Towards a Manpower Policy', John Wiley & Sons, Inc.

Mackay, D.I. & Others (1971), 'Labour Markets under Different Employment Conditions', George Allen & Unwin Ltd., London, 1971.

Magnum, Garth L. (1967), 'The National Programme', in Gordon, Robert A, Op. cit.

Majumdar, Bhaskar, (1995), 'Manpower Mobility in an Era of Globalization: Some Issues', *Productivity*, Vol. 36, No. 1, April-June.

——————, (2004), '*Sampoorna Grameen Rozgar Yojana* (Food for Work Component) Efficacy and Effectiveness', Report submitted to Planning Commission, GOI.

——————, (1997), "Accommodating New Economic Policy in India's Social Dynamics: A Critical Review", *Productivity*, Vol. 37, No. 4, Jan-March.

——————, (1990), 'Import Substituting Industrialization Strategy in India Economy: An Evaluation', The Indian Journal of Economics, Vol. XXXI, Part I, Oct.

——————, (2001), *Public Distribution System of Essential Commodities as a Social Safety Net: A Study of the District of Allahabad, Uttar Pradesh*, Report submitted to the Planning Commission, India.

——————, 2001, 'Technological Progress and Redundancy of Workers: Tasks for Rehabilitation', Labour & Development, Vol. 7, No. 2, Dec.

——————, 2004, 'Informalization of Global Labour and Survival of Local Workers', Productivity, Vol. 44, No. 4, Jan-March.

——————, 2004a, 'Living in Slums: A Study of the City of Allahabad, Uttar Pradesh', Mimeo, G. B. Pant Social Science Institute, Allahabad, India.

——————, 2005, 'Rural Housing and Living Condition of People Settled in Rural Uttar Pradesh: A Study', Report submitted to Planning Commission, Government of India.

Mascarenhas, R.C. (1982) 'Technology Trade and Development India's HMT Company, A West View Replica Ed., West view Press, Colorado.

Myers, Charles A (1954), 'Labour Mobility in Two countries', in E. W. Bakke & Others, Op Cit.

Myrdal, Gunnar (1982) 'Asian Drama: An Enquiry into the Poverty of Nations', Vol. III, Kalyani Publishers, New Delhi, 1982.

National Institute of Rural Development (NIRD) (1999), "India Rural Development Report", Hyderabad.

Nurkse, R. (1980), *Problems of Capital Formation in Under-developed Countries*, Oxford, Basil Blackwell.

Organization for Economic Cooperation and Development (OECD) (1965), 'Wages and Labour Mobility', Paris July.

Patnaik, P. (1984), "Market Question and Capitalist Development in India", *Economic and Political Weekly*, Vol. XIX, Annual Number, August.

Rameshan, P., (1998), 'Employment Reduction under Reforms and the Productivity of sick PSEs: A Learning Curve Analysis', *The Indian Journal of Labour Economics*, Vol. 41, No. 1, Jan-March.

Reddaway, W.B., (1968), 'Wage Flexibility and the Distribution of Labour', in McCormic B.J. & Smith, Owen E. (E.D.) The labour Market, Selected Reading, Penguin Books.

Reynolds, Lloyds (1951), *The Structure of Labour Market*, Harper & Brother, New York.

Rottenberg, 5. (1968), "On Choice in Labour Markets", in McCormic, B. J. and Smith, Owen, E (Ed), T*he Labour Market, Selected Readings*, Penguin Books.

Rowlery, Charles, (1980), 'Industrial Policy in the Mixed Economy' in Lord Roll of Ipsden (Ed), 'The Mixed Economy' Proceedings of Section F (Economics) of the British Association for the Advancement of Science), MacMillan Press, London.

Stewart, F., 1977, Technology and Underdevelopment, Macmillan.

Streeten, P. and S. J. Burki (1978), "Basic Needs: Some Issues", *World Development*, Vol. 6, No. 3.

Streeten, Paul, (1982), 'Approaches to a New International Economic Order', World Development, Vol. 10, No.1.

United Nations (1978), "The Significance of Rural Housing in Integrated Rural Development", Department of Economic and Social Affairs, New York.

Venkata Ratnam, C. S., (1998), 'Economic Reforms and Labour', *Productivity*, V. 39, No. 3, Oct-Dec.

World Bank (1978), "Rural Enterprise and Non-farm Employment", A World Bank Paper, January.

Index